MOVIE STARS
IN
BATHTUBS

MOVIE STARS IN BATHTUBS

by
Jack Scagnetti

JD | JONATHAN DAVID PUBLISHERS, INC.
   | MIDDLE VILLAGE, N.Y. 11379

MOVIE STARS IN BATHTUBS
by
Jack Scagnetti
Copyright © 1975
by
Jonathan David Publishers, Inc.

No part of this book may be reproduced in any manner or form without written permission from the publisher. Address all requests to:

Jonathan David Publishers
68-22 Eliot Avenue
Middle Village, New York 11379

Library of Congress Cataloging in Publication Data

Scagnetti, Jack.
   Movie stars in bathtubs.

  1.   Moving-picture actors and actresses—United States—Portraits. 2. Baths in moving-pictures.
I. Title.
PN1998.A2S3   791.43′028′0922   74-31216
ISBN 0-8426-0196-3

Printed in the United States of America

Acknowledgments

FOR THEIR KINDNESS and assistance, I offer special thanks to The Margaret Herrick Library of the Academy of Motion Pictures Arts and Sciences, Raymond Lee, Roy George Associates, Eddie Brandt's Saturday Matinee, Larry Edmunds Book Shop, Ray Trail, Richard Hudson, Loraine Burdick, and to the following motion picture studios: Universal, MGM, Paramount, Twentieth Century Fox, Columbia, Warner Brothers, and Walt Disney Productions.

J.S.

TABLE OF CONTENTS

Introduction 9

Part One
    THE FEMALE STARS 17

Part Two
    THE MALE STARS 61

Part Three
    MALES AND FEMALES TOGETHER 95

Part Four
    THE COMICS 119

Part Five
    CHILDREN AND ANIMALS 135

Index to Photographs 157

Charlie Chaplin prepares for a bathing scene in *A King in New York*, 1957 release filmed in England. The movie was produced, directed and written by Chaplin.

Introduction

OVER THE YEARS, movie scenes showing stars bathing or showering have become commonplace. Some of Hollywood's most memorable moments revolve about bathtubs. What we take for granted, however, took great pioneering effort by directors who set the stage for this development.

As far back as May, 1918, when the Famous Players-Lasky motion picture studios in Hollywood released a movie called *Old Wives for New,* film critics were outraged by some of the bath scenes.

Said one critic: "Disgusting debauchery . . . most immoral episodes."

Said another: "Classy . . . but rough in spots."

Others reacted more favorably: "It at least shows that the photoplay is breaking away from the marshmallow school of drama," said one. "A splendid story . . . faultlessly produced, carrying a powerful sermon," commented a second critic.

Silent films were made in the days when the mood of America was still quite puritanical—just a few years before the changing trends that came with the Roaring Twenties. These movies started with stories depicting a lazy and slovenly wife destroying her marriage. Such a story provided the setting for director Cecil B. DeMille's first bath scene.

Elliott Dexter, playing the role of the wronged husband, was shown trying to shave in a messy bathroom, littered with dirty clothes. Sylvia Ashton, as Sophy

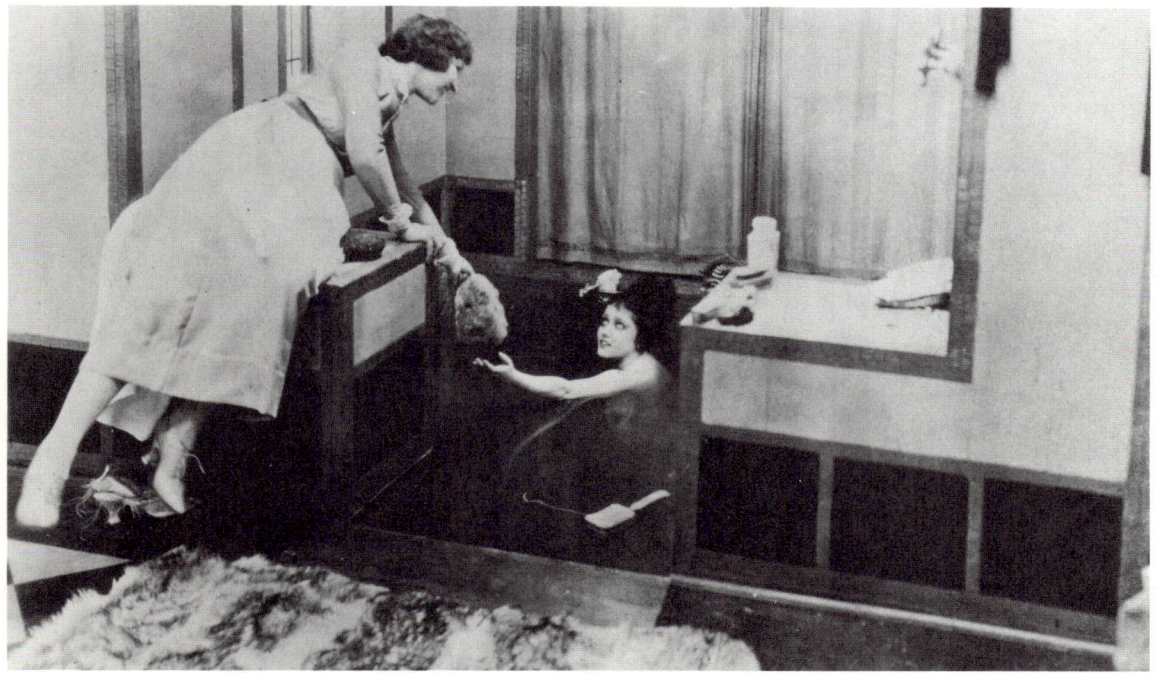

Gloria Swanson takes a bath in what is Hollywood's first motion picture bathing scene. It was in the film, *Male and Female,* directed by Cecil B. DeMille in 1919.

Murdock, the housewife, played her part very realistically—so much so that some film critics commented years later that "had the Academy Awards been in existence, Sylvia Ashton would have won an Oscar for her loathsome performance."

This bathroom scene was designed to reveal the housewife's character and habits, and to explain why a husband might become disloyal and find himself attracted to a neat, fastidious and lovely "other" woman. It was the inaugural for a series of similar episodes that DeMille would include in the many films he was to produce and direct during the next four decades.

Press agents latched on to the theme that DeMille's fame as a director was due, in great measure, to his having conceived the idea of using many different kinds of bathtub scenes in his productions.

DeMille reacted to this view by admitting that the bathtub and bathroom scenes in many of his pictures helped further his fame and career. But he also made the point that if America's bathrooms are cleaner and more comfortable

Through the years, bathing scenes have become popular in films and have included many in which men appeared. *Forty Guns*, a 20th Century Fox western, is one such movie.

today, perhaps his pictures had something to do with that development.

DeMille once remarked that he recalled the days when indoor sanitation was something of a novelty, and so, when he had an opportunity in later years to show on the screen that a bathroom could be clean, comfortable and bright, he

Sex queens of films, such as Jayne Mansfield were usually filmed in luxurious bubble baths, but occasionally the setting was less exotic. However, the scene was always exciting and pleasing to the viewer.

seized it. He believed very sincerely that he played a significant role in improving the American standard of living.

A year after the release of *Old Wives for New,* DeMille decided to glamorize a bathtub scene. Beautiful Gloria Swanson, who was to become one of the silent screen's truly great stars, was photographed taking a bath in *Male and Female.* It had taken DeMille quite a bit of coaxing to get the young actress to do the scene. He spared nothing to make things more comfortable for her. Security guards were posted around the set; anyone who was not in the scene was barred from the premises.

Gloria was draped in a silk towelette with fringe, and was assisted by two maids. DeMille urged her to prolong the bath scene because it was, he felt, a

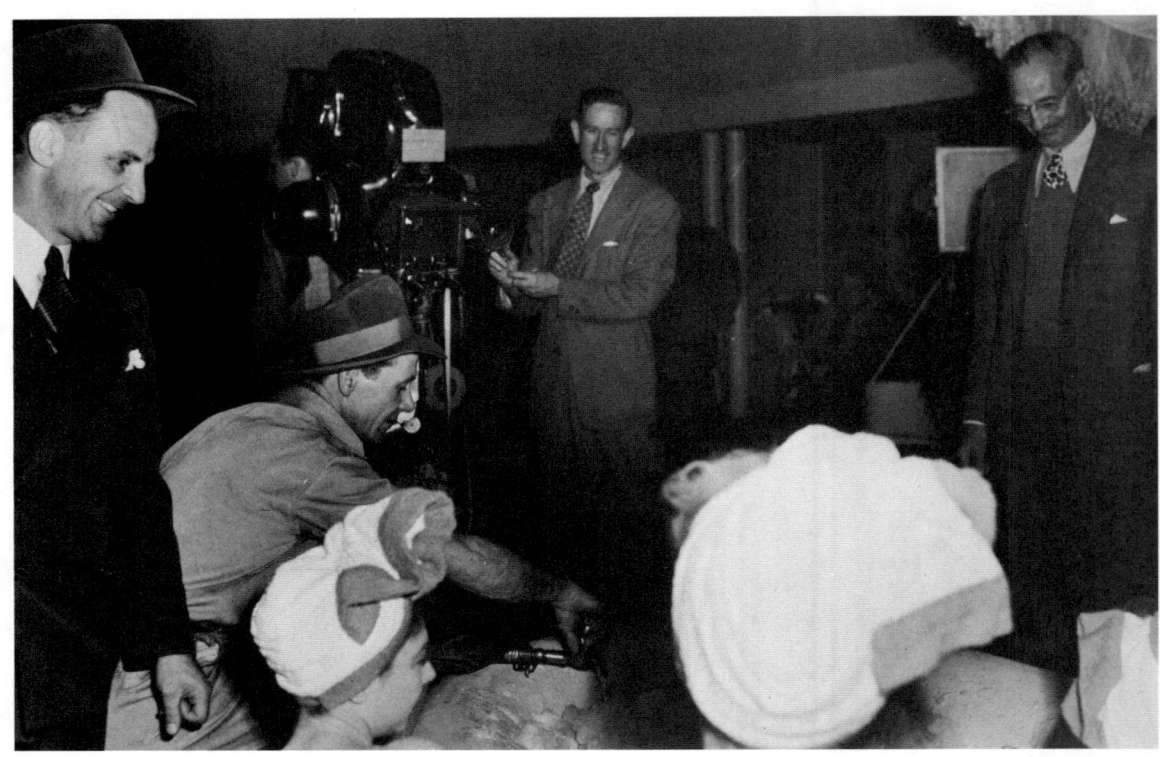

A bubble bath is filled for Gloria DeHaven's RKO film, *Step Lively*. A special mixture of effervescent liquid is poured in and cameramen get set for the perfect angle. Gloria DeHaven (with turban towel) watches carefully to make sure bubbles are not too transparent.

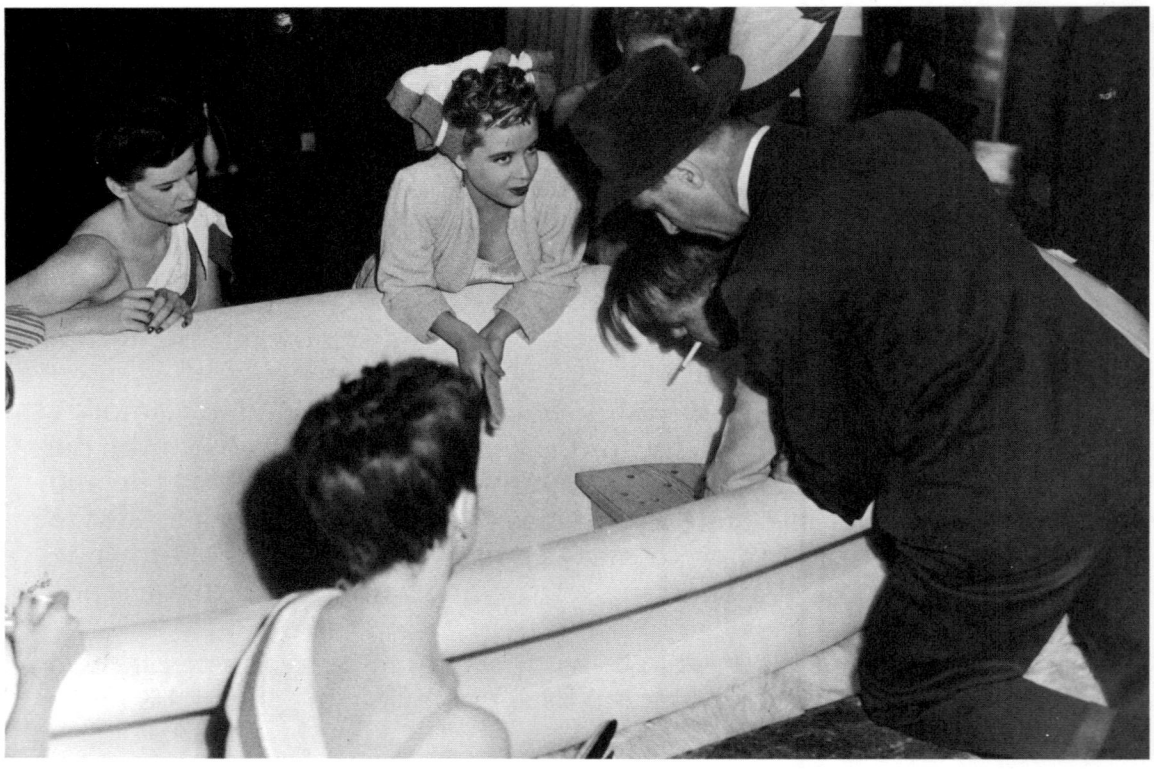

memorable highlight of the film. Such lingering bathing scenes, featuring either the heroine or the hero, became standard procedure for almost all DeMille films.

Approximately four decades later, Richard Griffith and Arthur Mayer wrote the following about the man who introduced the bathtub to the screen:

> Having decided to demote the gods and goddesses of the screen to ordinary human beings, DeMille began to analyze ordinary everyday life and probe it for situations which could be made more attractive. His first discovery was the bathroom.
>
> To a generation brought up never to mention personal sanitation, he introduced bathing as an art and disrobing as a prolonged rapture. In the shrine of cleanliness, even partial nudity was so obvious a necessity that the most godly could not object to their display on the screen.

A scene identification sign is set up prior to shooting a bathroom scene in a film directed by Gregory Ratoff.

DeMille's glorification of the bath probably did much to make the traditional Saturday night immersion more of a weekly ritual in the American home.

In one of his early spectacles, *The Sign of the Cross*, starring Claudette Colbert and Charles Laughton, DeMille again featured a bathing scene. Playing

Sex-oriented films find bathtubs useful as focal points for scenes. Above, a scene from *Beyond the Valley of the Dolls.* Below, a scene from *Last Tango in Paris,* featuring Maria Schneider, and starring Marlon Brando.

Poppaea, Nero's wife, Claudette bathed in a huge tub. So that the actress would sense the feeling of luxury and affluence, DeMille saw to it that the tub was filled with asses' warm milk.

The humorous potential of bathtub scenes was first recognized in films starring Charlie Chaplin, Laurel & Hardy, Fatty Arbuckle, Buster Keaton, Harold Lloyd, the Marx Brothers, the Three Stooges, and continued through the years with modern comedians.

Until recent years, of course, the camera always cut short (or cut out) any scenes containing frontal nudity. Today much more of the human body is bared.

Great drama has been added to the screen through bathtub scenes. Films depicting horror and murder, such as the Alfred Hitchcock thriller, *Psycho*, made use of the shower or the bath to build up suspense. Such scenes portraying violence have not been included in this volume. The most violent scene we present is a mild slapping scene (James Cagney slapping a man under a shower).

While most of the movie scenes showing female stars in bathtubs or showers have been sexy siren types, Hollywood films have had their share of pictures in which sophisticated actresses are shown bathing—women like Greer Garson, Deborah Kerr, Merle Oberon and Olivia de Havilland.

Even the sophisticated Lynn Fontanne, the celebrated stage star and wife of Alfred Lunt, appeared in a nude bathing scene. It was in the film *The Guardsman*. On the day of the shooting, Mr. Lunt showed up on the set, although he wasn't scheduled to be in the scene. He came to help bolster his wife's morale.

According to the script, Miss Fontanne was to go to the tub, step in, and then, as the cameras moved away from her, the maid was to remove her robe.

But Miss Fontanne had other ideas. When the scene was actually shot, instead of handing the robe to the maid, she dropped it beside the tub—much to the surprise of director Sidney Franklin, members of the cast, and the film crew.

Then, Miss Fontanne's beautiful voice rang across the sound stage: "Ladies and gentlemen, when I am called to do a scene, I do it. As you all know, no one takes a bath with a robe on."

Her husband stepped beside her quickly, and picking up the robe, said, "My wife and I always try to make things as true to life as possible."

One of the great directors of the early days of moviemaking who strove for realism was Erich Von Stroheim. He has often been called "Hollywood's greatest realist." Although recognized as an artist who wanted to photograph life as it is, regardless of cost, his career as a director was short-lived, and he was eventually compelled to move into the realm of acting.

In his 1919 sex drama, *The Devil's Passkey*, he included a ceramic bath caper for Mae Busch, who was not only famous for her talent, but for her temper tantrums. In the scene, which called for a sunken marble bathtub (which critics later called "the high-water mark of the film"), she was to step daintily into the Romanesque tub. But, as she stepped down the stairs, she slipped on some soap, and fell head back against the side of the tub. She was bleeding from a cut on her neck as Von Stroheim screamed for a doctor. The cut was minor, but Mae shouted in her best Australian accent: "My God! This is real marble. I could have been killed!"

Assisting Mae to a chair, Stroheim said, "Miss Busch, all things are real in a Von Stroheim film!"

Von Stroheim created another memorable bath scene. This one was in 1928 in *Queen Kelly*. Seena Owen, playing a wild character who was walking—completely naked—around a palace, with a beautiful white cat on her shoulder, appeared in a bath scene. She had the cat on her shoulder, while a maid gave her a pedicure.

Everything went wrong! Von Stroheim was very upset that day. The cat sneezed too much. So three other cats were brought in. The maid cut herself as she manicured Seena's toe nails. And, as Seena started to get out of the tub, she fell and struck her head on the marble and passed out. It seemed like a rerun of the Mae Busch caper.

In the pages of this book, you will find scores of enjoyable and memorable movie bathing scenes—some going back to the silent screen era. There are gorgeous females, handsome males, some delightful scenes of male and females together, comedians, children and animals.

All of what follows is presented as good, clean fun, and as a bit of the interesting side of movie memories so precious to many Americans.

JACK SCAGNETTI

1
The Female Stars

Paramount's 1962 release, *Who's Got the Action?*, starring Dean Martin and Lana Turner, featured this scene of Lana typing in the tub. Co-starring in the movie were Eddie Albert, Walter Matthau and Paul Ford.

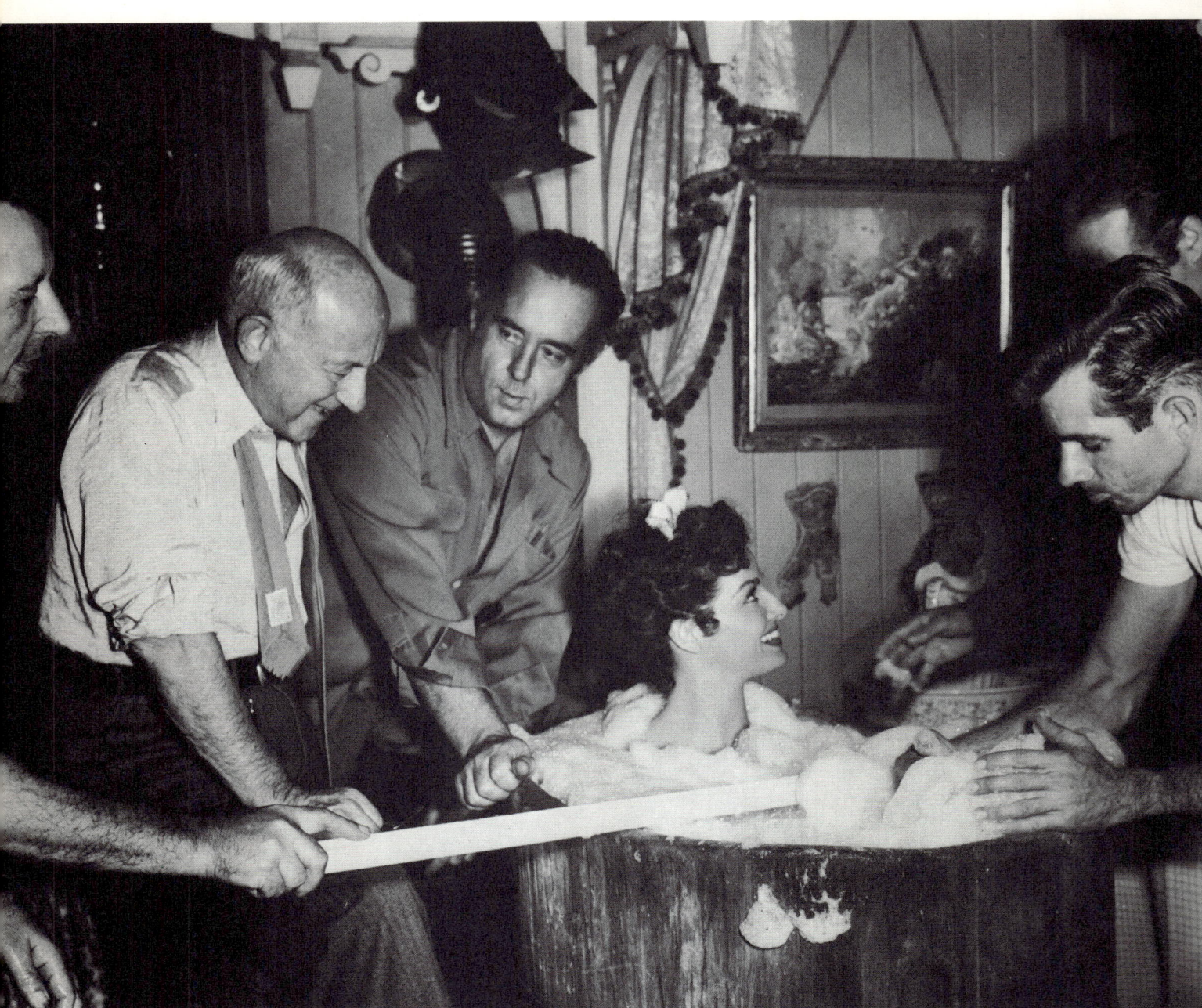

Since Jane Russell used the same wooden barrel that Paulette Goddard used in Cecil B. DeMille's *Unconquered,* director Frank Tashlin and producer Robert Welch invited DeMille to act as a technical adviser on this scene from *Son of Paleface.*

Here's a closeup view of Jane Russell, smiling for the camera in *Son of Paleface*, as soap suds start to rise.

Gloria DeHaven takes the plunge in RKO Radio's film, *Step Lively*.

(Above) Director Tim Whelan shapes suds with a smoothing board in *Step Lively*. Assistant removes a bubble from Gloria DeHaven's eye, while another tests temperature of water. (Below) The head electrician checks the density of the set lights. Suds are blown in through a special nozzle.

Jayne Mansfield reads *Peyton Place* in this sudsy scene from the 20th Century Fox production, *Will Success Spoil Rock Hunter?* Joan Blondell looks on.

Publicity shot of Jayne Mansfield shows her bathing in a fun-loving mood aboard cruise ship *SS Independence*.

Mamie VanDoren, popular sex symbol during the 1960s, tries showering without *wetting her hair*.

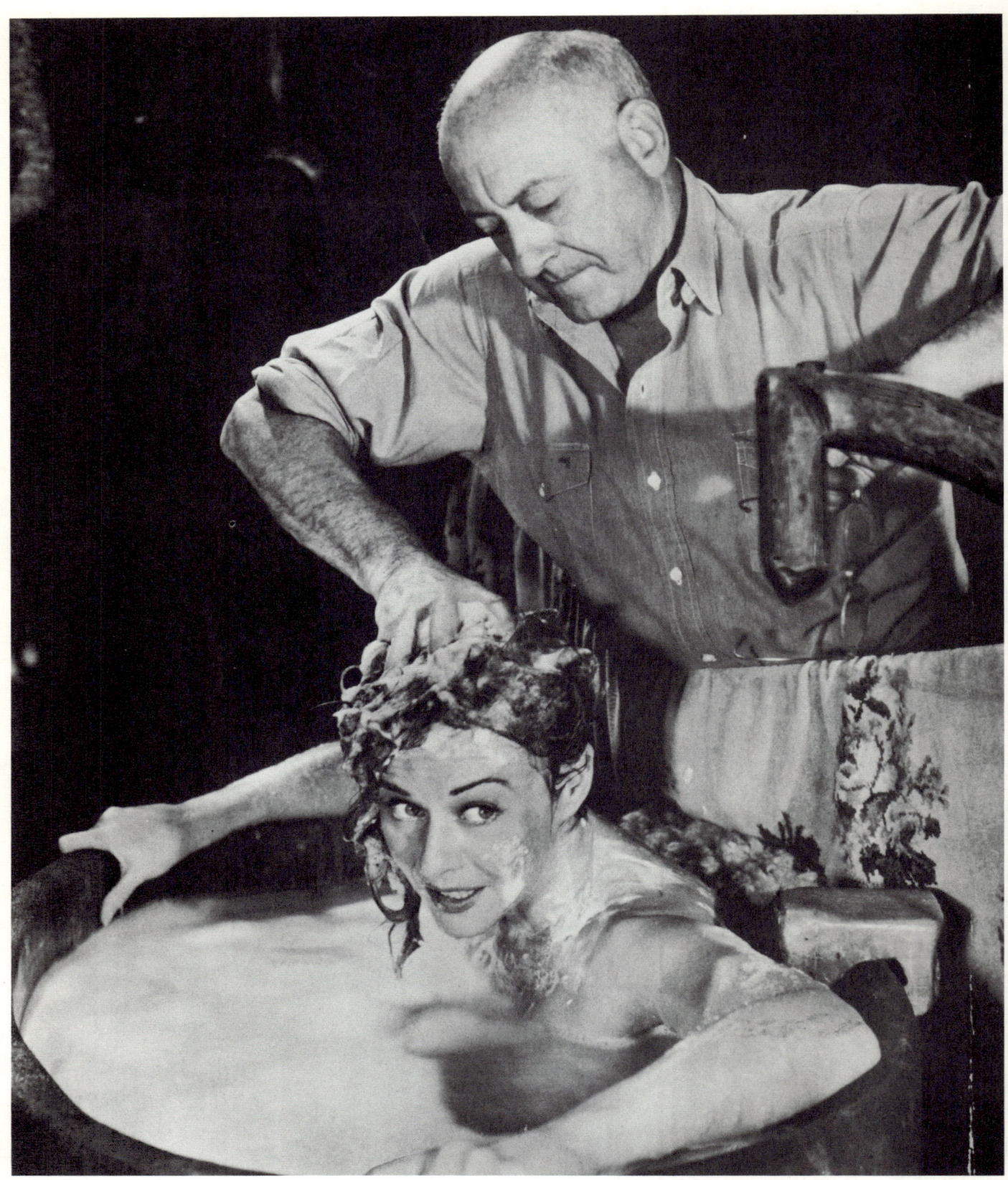

Cecil B. DeMille, who is credited with starting the trend of bathing scenes in motion pictures, prepared Paulette Goddard for a scene in *Unconquered*, a 1947 Paramount release.

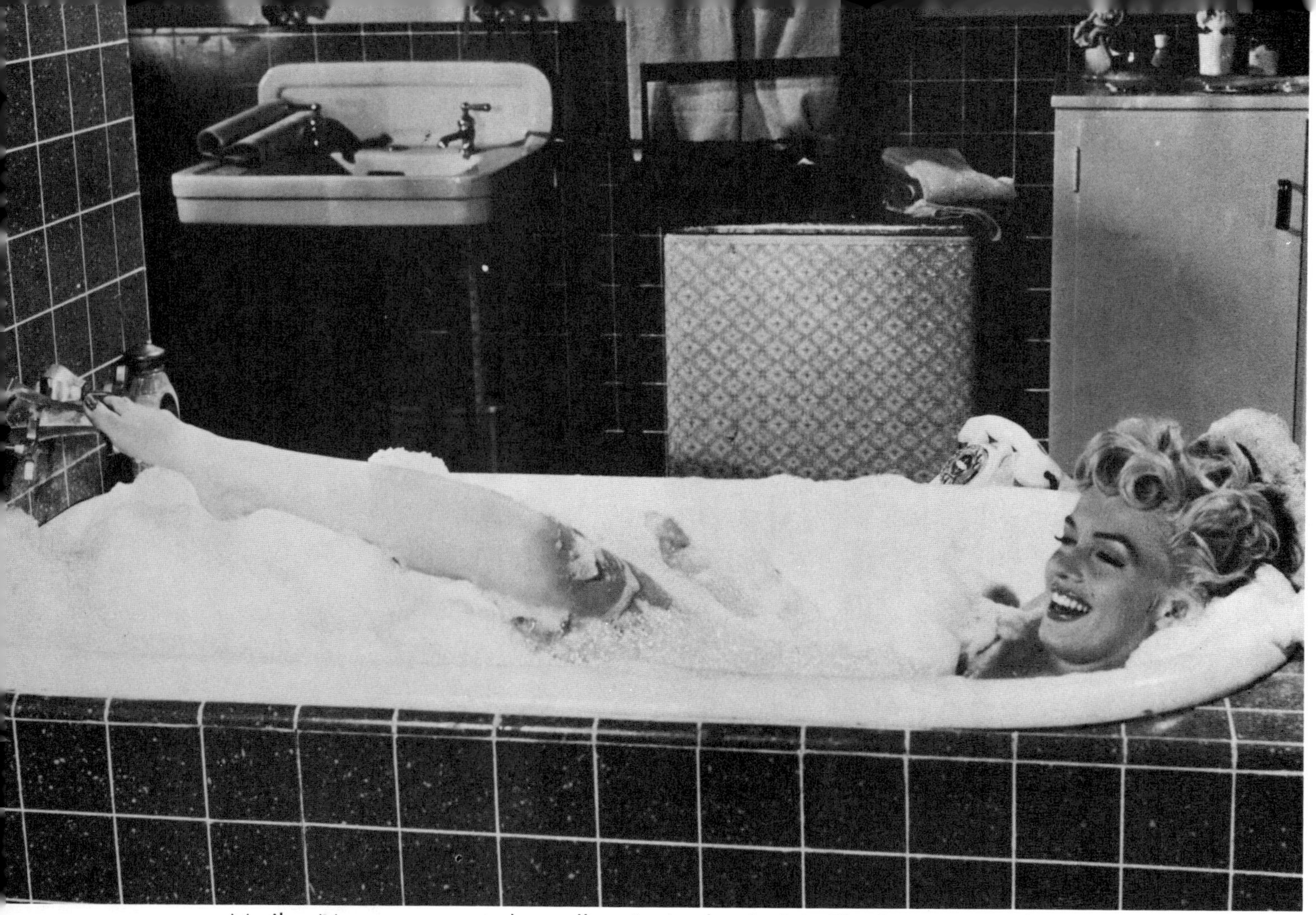

Marilyn Monroe seems to be really enjoying her bath in *The Seven Year Itch,* a 1955 production of 20th Century Fox, co-starring Tom Ewell.

Telephones always seem to ring when one is bathing, as Jean Simmons shows in *The Grass Is Greener,* a 1960 Universal International movie co-starring Cary Grant, Deborah Kerr and Robert Mitchum.

Columbia Pictures' publicity shot of Kim Novak in 1957 has the actress reading the comics in the bathtub.

An antique French tub is used by Lana Turner in the MGM musical, *The Merry Widow*, produced by Joe Pasternak. The 1952 film co-starred Fernando Lamas. (Inset) Lana Turner, wearing a necklace, earrings and ribbon, smiles happily in a scene from a 1941 film, *Ziegfeld Girl*.

Linda Darnell, a popular star in the 1940s and 1950s, expresses surprise in this scene from *Forever Amber*, a 20th Century Fox production.

Adornments decorate the elaborate tub Elizabeth Taylor uses in *Cleopatra*, the epic 1964 film about the famous Egyptian ruler.

Elizabeth Taylor and Mia Farrow (holding toy duck) have plenty of room to relax in this spacious tub in *The Secret Ceremony*. Robert Mitchum co-starred.

Sign of the Cross, a 1932 Paramount release, was one of Cecil B. DeMille's early bathing scenes. This one starred Claudette Colbert who, two years later, appeared in DeMille's *Cleopatra*.

Glynis Johns, lovely British film actress, plays a troublesome mermaid heroine in the comedy film, *Miranda*.

It's an elegant tub for Gina Lollobrigida in *Solomon and Sheba,* a United Artists release, co-starring Yul Brynner.

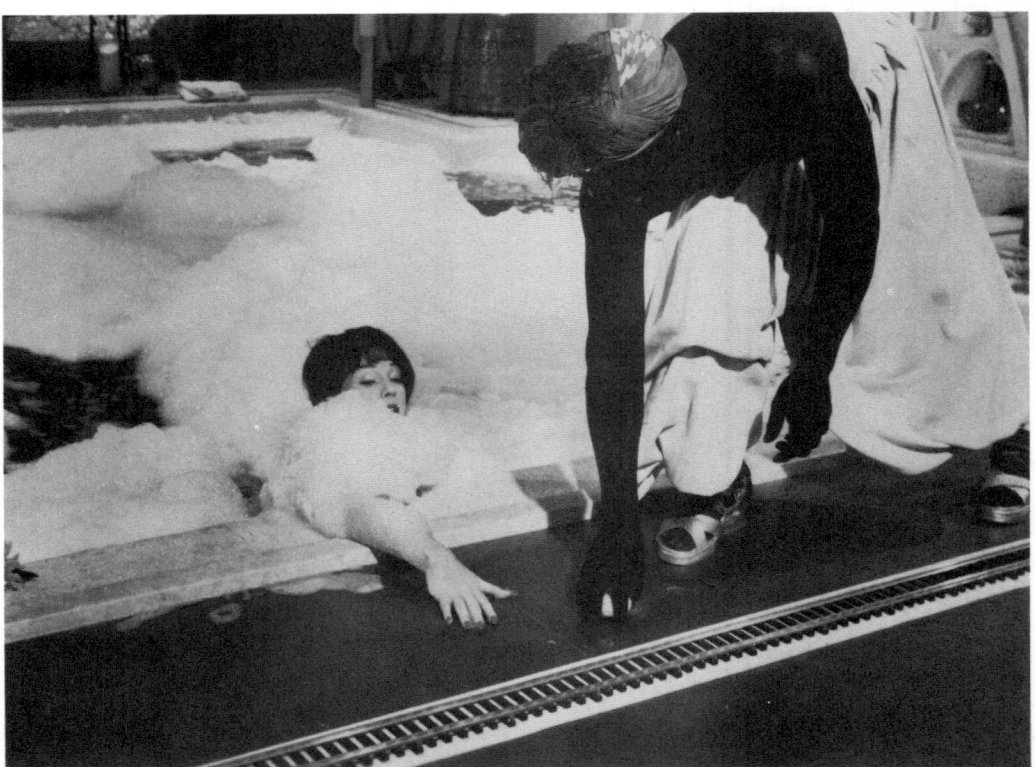

Shirley MacLaine needs some help when she can't reach a bar of soap in this scene from *John Goldfarb, Please Come Home!*

(Top) Deanna Durbin submerges herself in soap suds as she prepares for a bathing scene in *Can't Help Singing*. The bottom half of an old wine vat was used for the bathtub. (Bottom) Cameraman takes a reading on his light meter.

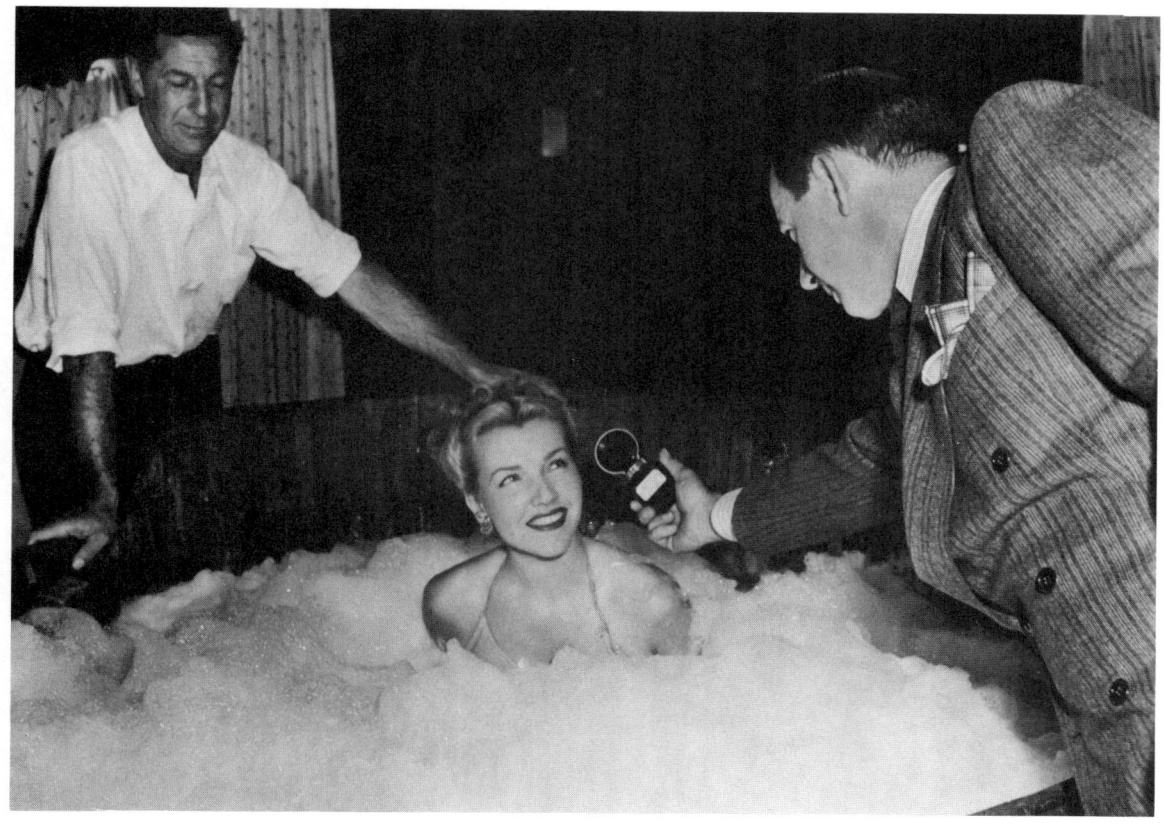

Maria Montez gets a last-minute makeup check for a scene in Universal's *Ali Baba and the Forty Thieves*.

Punkins Parker, winsome blonde, is one of 47 gorgeous girls who participate in a beauty ritual in *Artists and Models Abroad*. Behind Punkins is Claire James (seated) and Margie Medford (standing).

Natalie Wood finds comfort in this bathtub in *Love With a Proper Stranger*, co-starring Steve McQueen, Edie Adams and Herschel Bernardi.

Columbia's film about Old Baghdad, *A Thousand and One Nights,* features Evelyn Keyes as a pretty sight in a bubble bath.

Susan Hayward is served by two maids in the beautiful biblical film, *David and Bathsheba,* a 20th Century Fox production.

Romy Schneider receives a bouquet of flowers as she emerges from a shower in *Good Neighbor Sam*, a 1964 Columbia Pictures film.

Enjoying a shower in *Judith,* a Paramount Pictures release, is Italian sex siren Sophia Loren. Peter Finch and John Hawkins co-starred in this 1965 film.

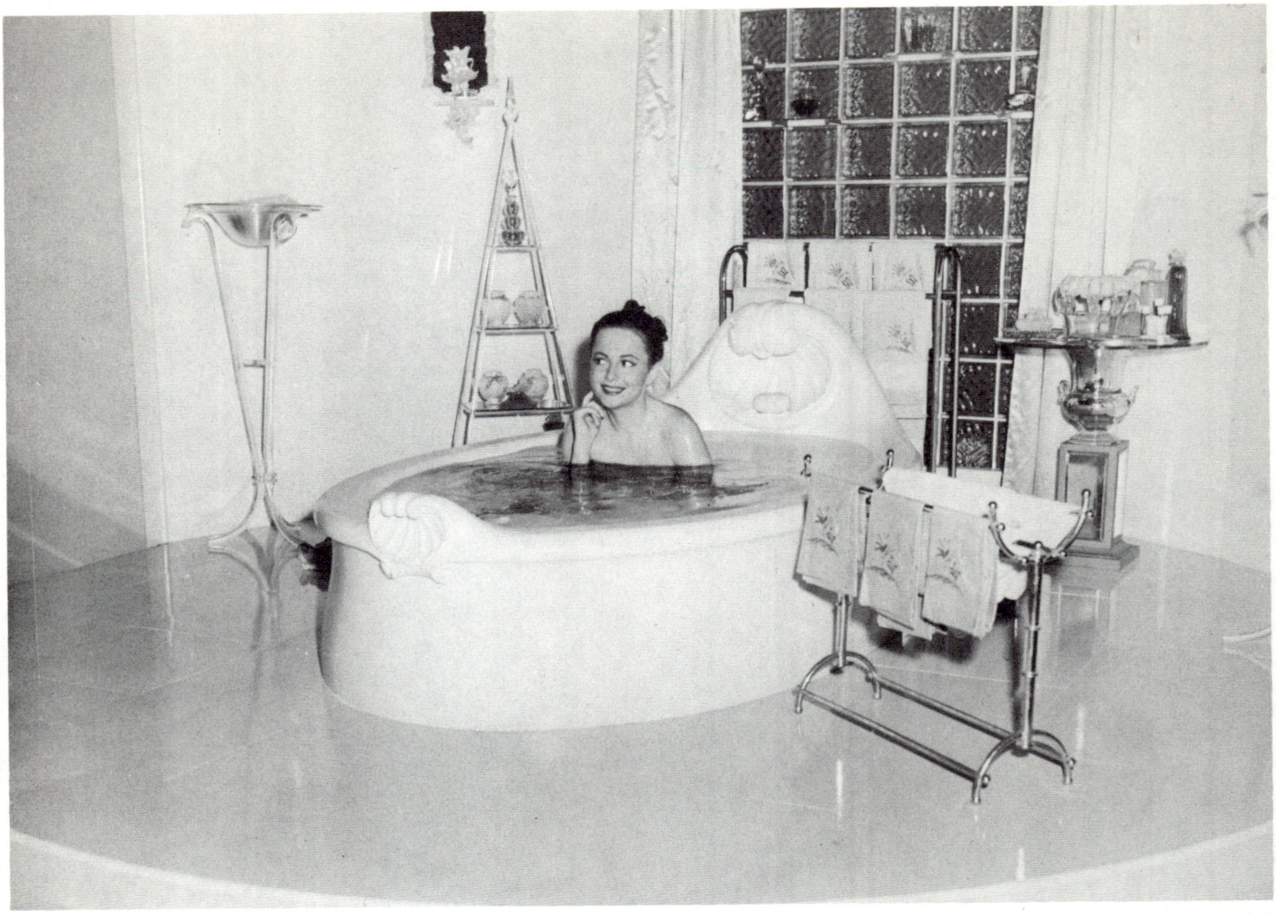

It's a classy bathtub for Olivia de Havilland in the 1942 Warner Brothers-First National picture film, *Princess O'Rourke*.

Greer Garson takes a sparkling bubble bath in MGM's *Julia Misbehaves*. Co-starring with her was Walter Pidgeon.

Judy Holiday, popular as the daffy blonde of the 1950s, in a 1960 film, *The Bells Are Ringing*.

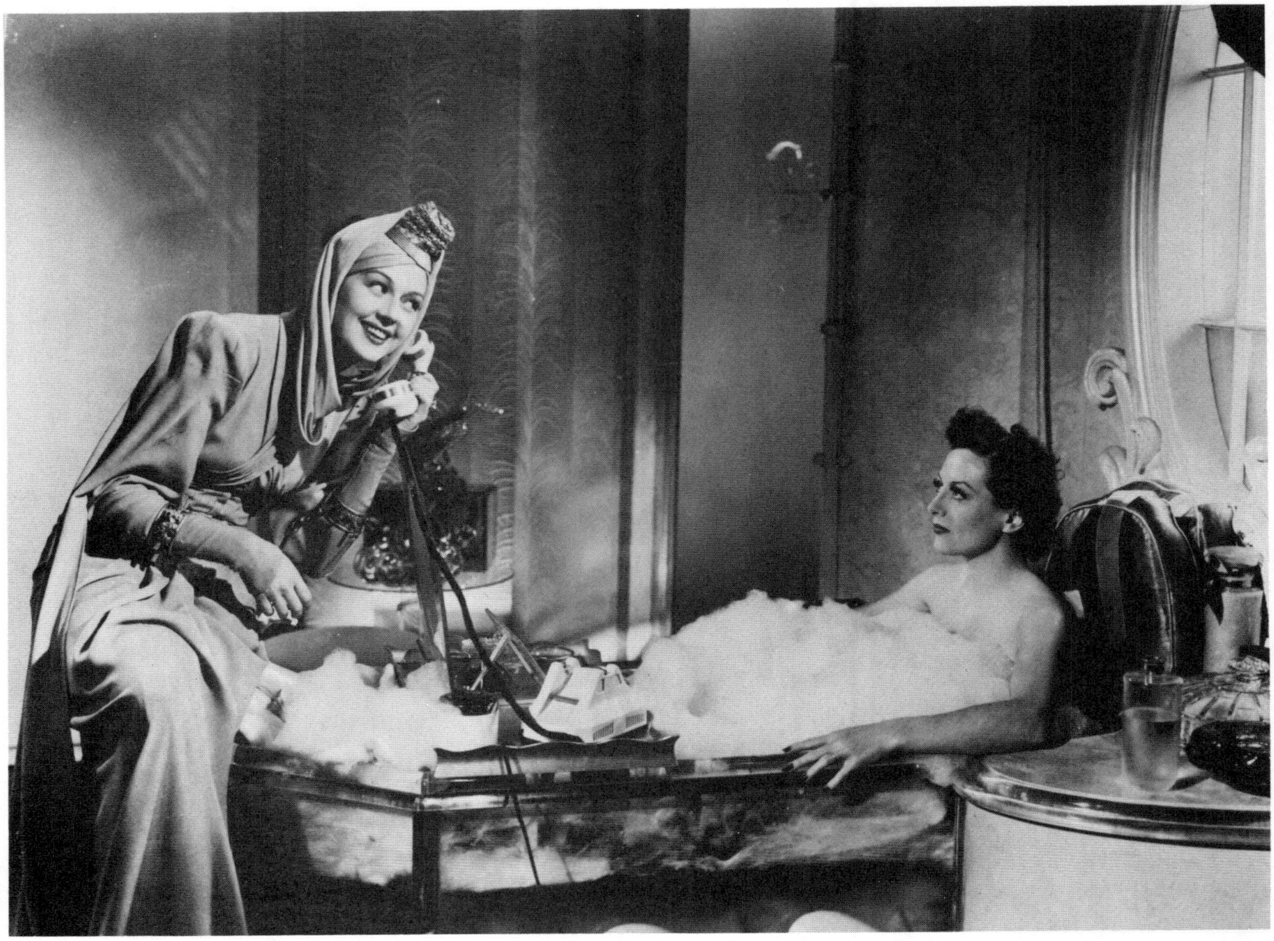

Rosalind Russell takes a telephone call while Joan Crawford listens intently while sitting in the bathtub in *The Women*.

Betty Grable sings in the bathtub in this scene from *Sweet Rosie O'Grady*.

Ann Sheridan, star of many films in the 1940s and 1950s, was called "The Oomph Girl" because of her sex appeal. Here she is in one of her screen roles.

Judy Garland sings while she takes a shower in the MGM musical, *Summer Stock*, co-starring Gene Kelly.

Deborah Kerr enjoys a hot bath in her tent (in a tub previously belonging to the Aga Khan) during filming of *King Solomon's Mines*.

Lois Maxwell prepares for a luxurious bath with the help of servants in Verdi's *Aida*, the first color opera-film. It was a 1954 Sol Hurok presentation.

Jill St. John enjoys a bubble bath in this scene from *The Liquidator,* MGM's screen version of John Gardner's best-selling, tongue-in-cheek spy thriller.

Marlene Dietrich's famous pretty legs don't show in this bubble bath scene, but her striking face attracts plenty of interest.

Lois Moran's job was to publicize soap in *Publicity Madness,* a film about the 1920s.

Gena Rowlands steps out from a shower in *Bay the Moon,* a 1957 MGM comedy co-starring Jim Backus. Jose Ferrer starred in and directed the film.

Mitsuko Kimura, lovely Japanese actress, in a typical Japanese bathtub. The scene is from Columbia's 1955 film, *Sergeant O'Reilly,* in which she played the feminine lead opposite Aldo Ray.

(Left) Caked with "beauty mud," Nancy Carroll is preparing for a shower in *Personal Maid*, a 1931 Paramount Pictures movie.

(Below) Jeanette MacDonald, American concert singer and a leading lady in musical films during the 1930s, in a scene from *Annabelle's Affairs*, a 1931 release. She appeared in a series of film operettas wth Nelson Eddy.

Beautiful bubbles fill the air as Vera Ralston poses in a small, metal tub for a studio publicity pose.

Lucille Bremer smiles happily when she receives a call from Fred Astaire who asks her for a date. Fred is a debonair rogue who poses as her guardian angel in order to swindle her.

(Above) Taina Elg, in a bathtub from a sequence in MGM's *Imitation General*. She relaxes between scenes in this 1958 film with Glenn Ford.

(Below) Joan Collins, in MGM's 1956 *The Opposite Sex,* takes a bubble bath in a jade-green plastic tub fashioned to look like a huge Lalique crystal. Fixtures are gold-plated with the water spout in the shape of a swan and with serpentine handles.

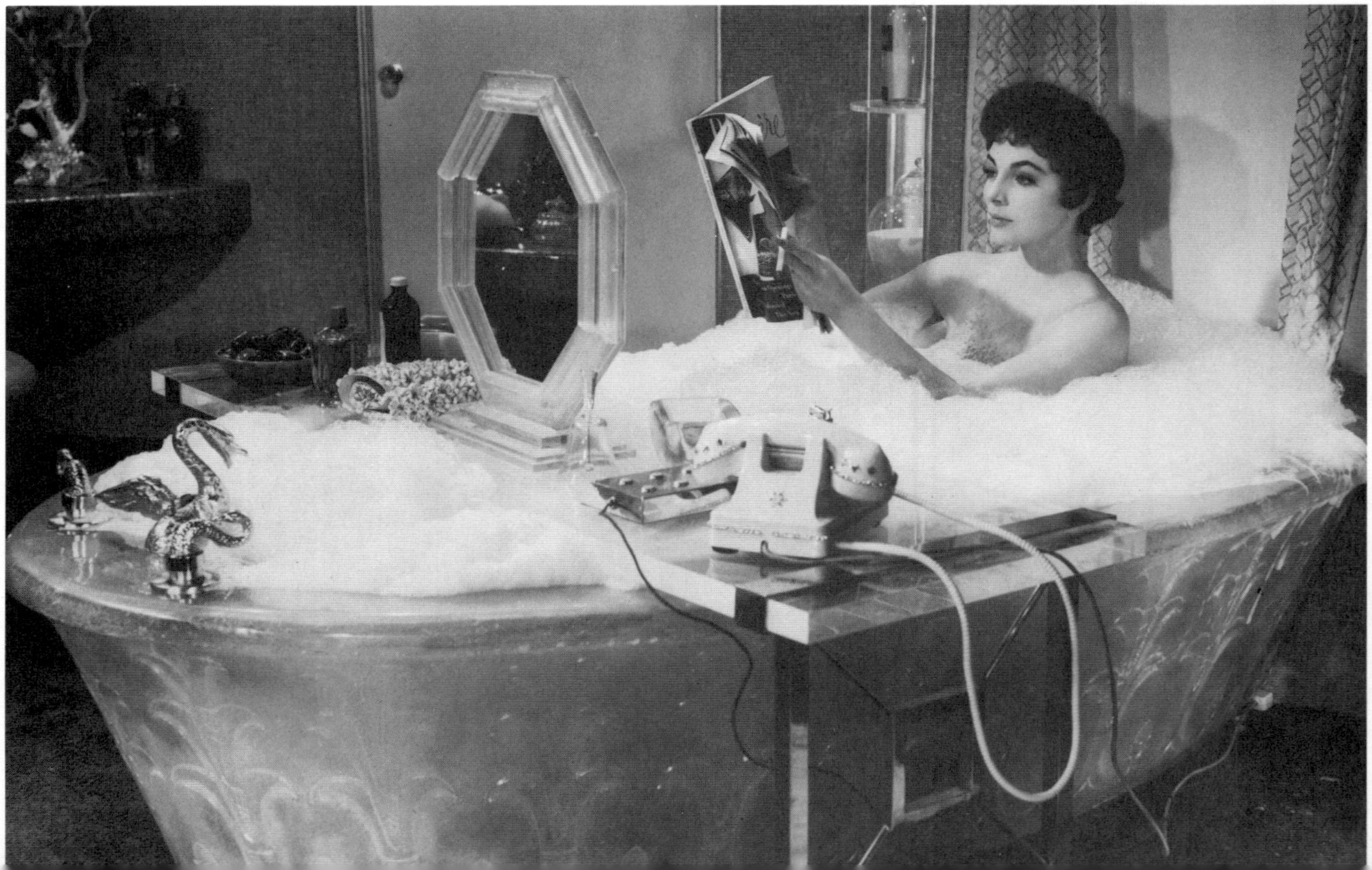

Ruth Hussey enjoys a bath after she is discharged from prison, while Rita Johnson, her former cellmate, helps in the luxurious process in MGM's 1939 release, *Within the Law*.

Deborah Kerr is a conservative British war bride in *Count Your Blessings*, a 1958 MGM release. Martin Stephens hands her a towel which was out of reach.

One of Hollywood's most famous models and cover girls of the 1940s, Patricia Mace, poses in a tub for Universal Studios' publicity prior to her first film, *Cobra Woman*. She plays a lady-in-waiting to Maria Montez.

Marion Davies, famous star of the silent screen era, promotes plumbers and bathtubs in *Five O'Clock Girl*.

Norma Shearer was filmed in bathroom scenes in *After Midnight,* a 1921 film.

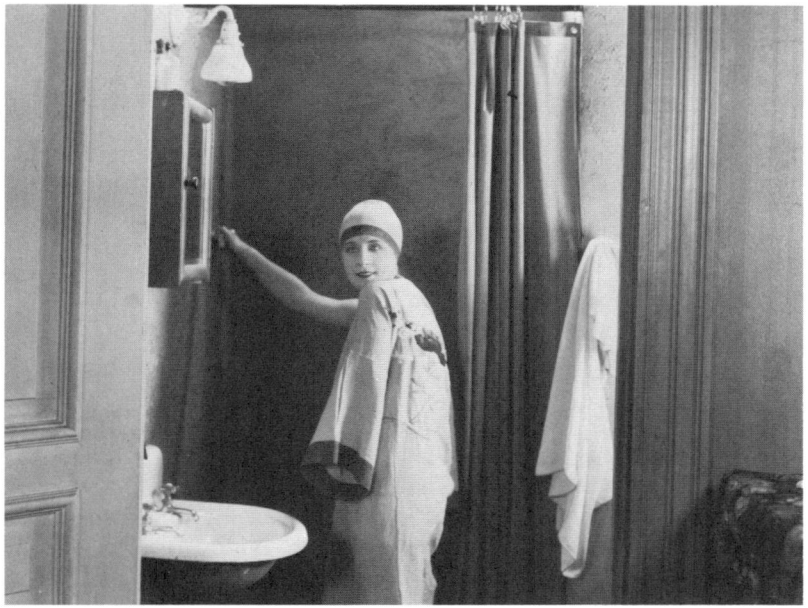

Ellen Drew cools off in her own handmade shower in this 1944 shot. She uses ice water because the temperatures in Hollywood were near the 100° mark.

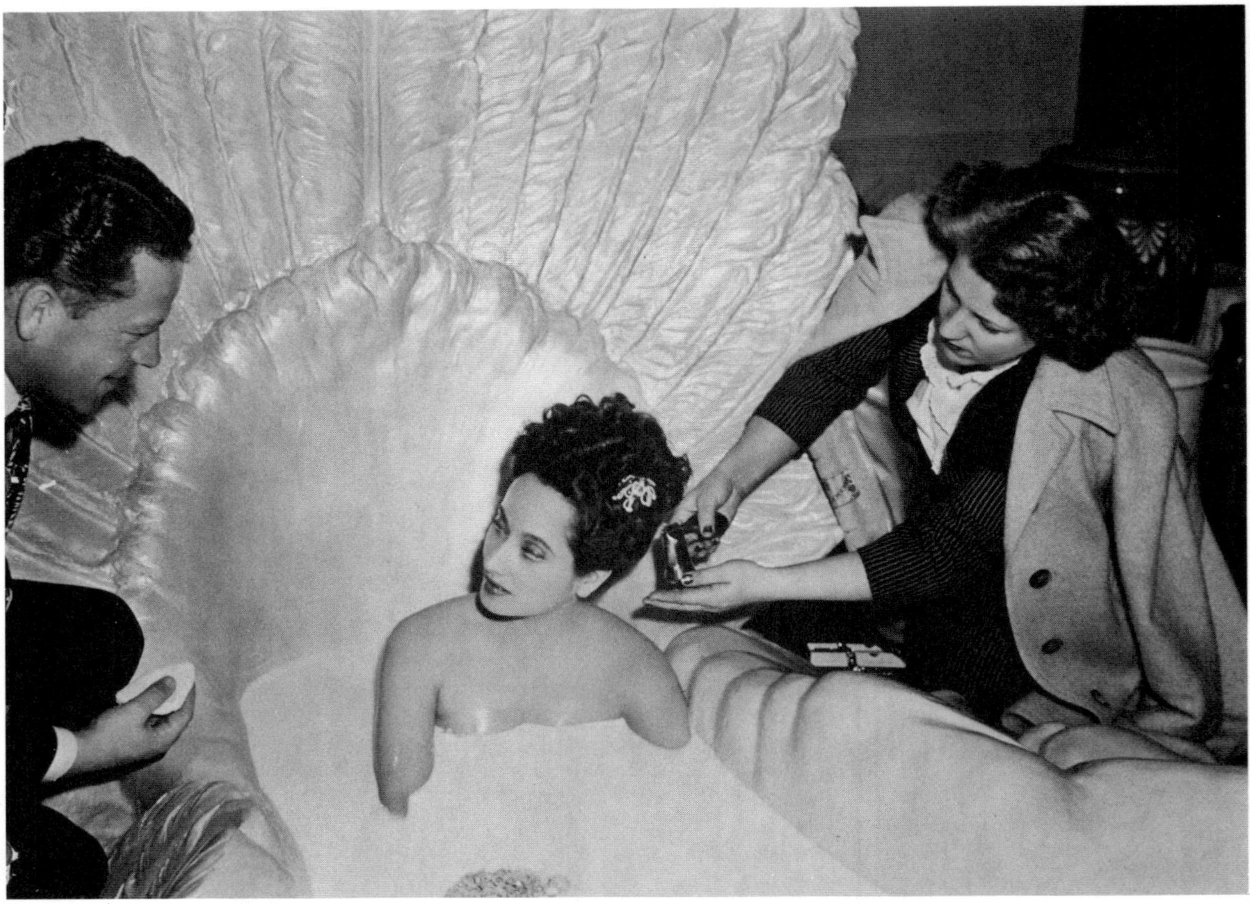

Merle Oberon receives the personal attention of her hairdresser and her makeup man in this ornate tub in the 1945 film, *Night in Paradise*.

The identity of this actress remains unknown despite a thorough search of the records. The photo is reportedly from a scene in *A Man's World,* a 1918 or 1924 film.

Wendy Hiller, in Bernard Shaw's screen version of *Pygmalion*, is required to take a bath as she changes from a girl of the gutter to an acceptable member of royal society. Her bath scene is one of the highly amusing incidents in the movie.

Marjorie Main relaxes her tired feet after dancing all night in *The Law and Lady Loverly*, a sophisticated comedy of the 1950 era.

2
The Male Stars

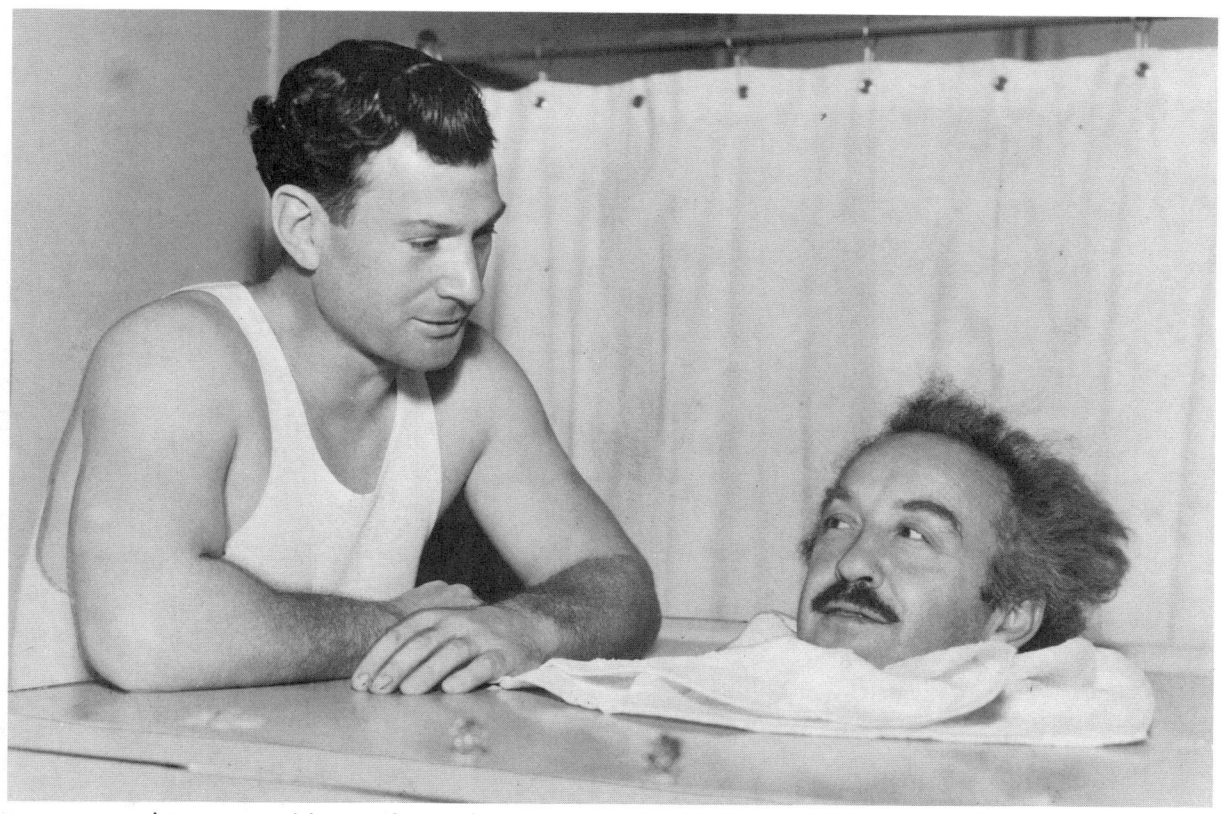

This 1934 publicity photo shows where the Hollywood film, *Man Alive*, germinated. Masseur James Davies (left) reveals a story idea to J. P. McEvoy, a playwright, while he was soaking in the Paramount gymnasium.

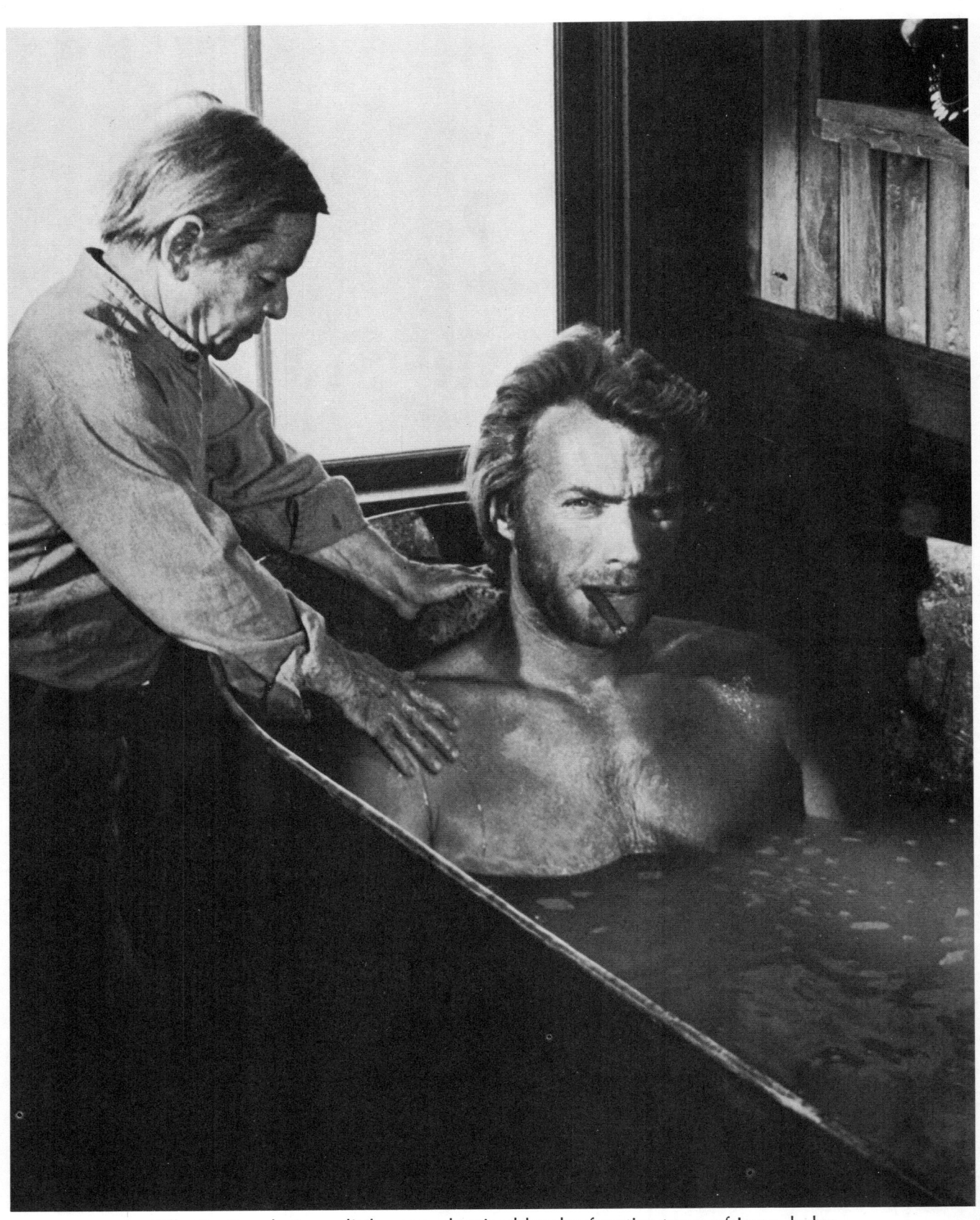
Billy Curtis, playing a little man, despised by the frontier town of Lago, helps Clint Eastwood when he visits the local barber shop in *High Plains Drifter*.

A halfway "closed" set (women were barred) was ordered by Universal Pictures when Paul Newman took a bath in *The Secret War of Harry Frigg*.

Jack Lemmon seems concerned with what Walter Matthau has rigged up for him in the bathtub in this scene from *The Fortune Cookie*.

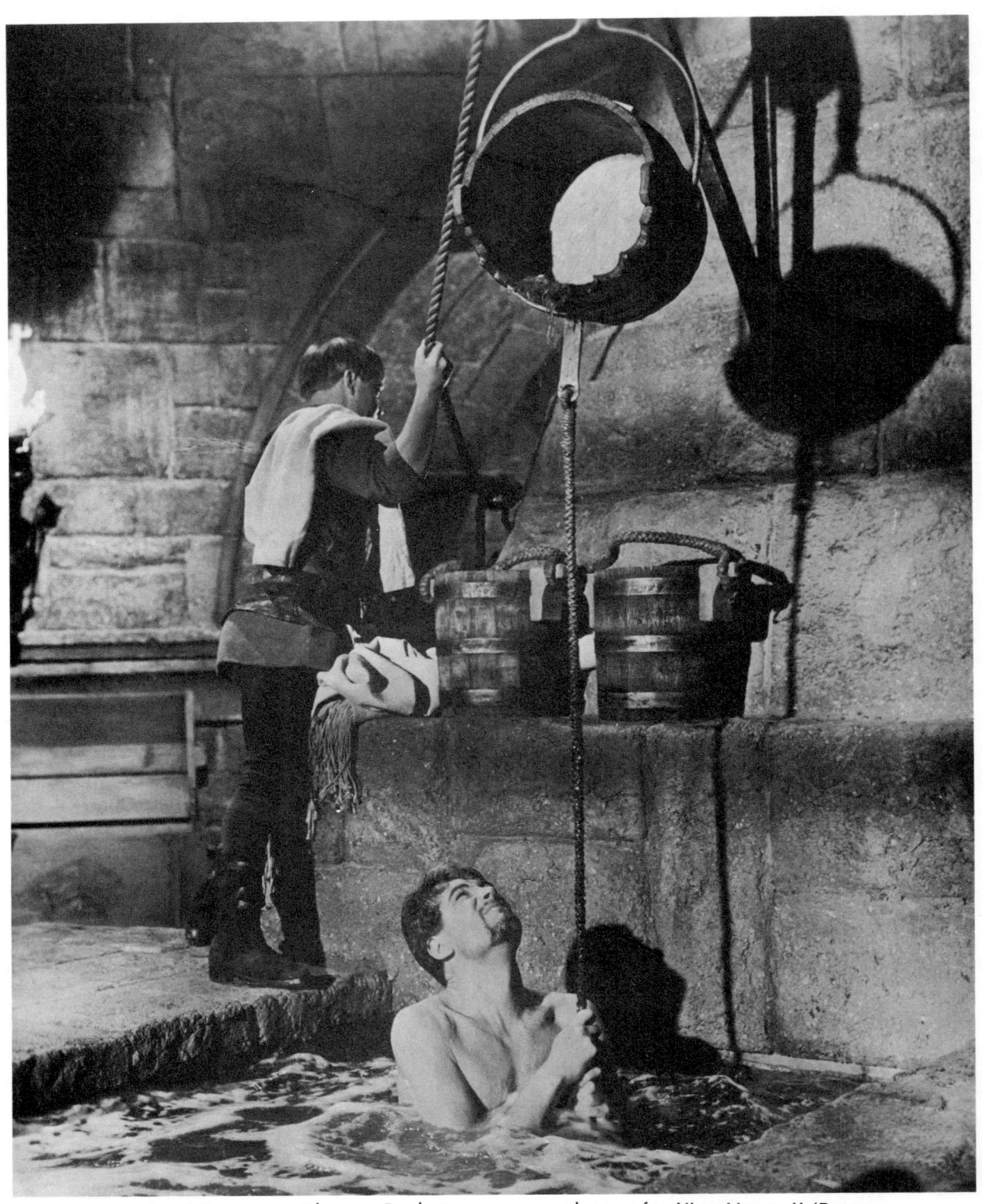
Richard Burton, as Thomas Becket, prepares a shower for King Henry II (Peter O'Toole) in *Becket*.

Peter O'Toole, as King Henry II in *Becket*, takes a shower.

(Above) Peter O'Toole, is dried off by Richard Burton in *Becket*, a Hal Wallis production released by Paramount. (Below) Burton assists O'Toole in getting dressed.

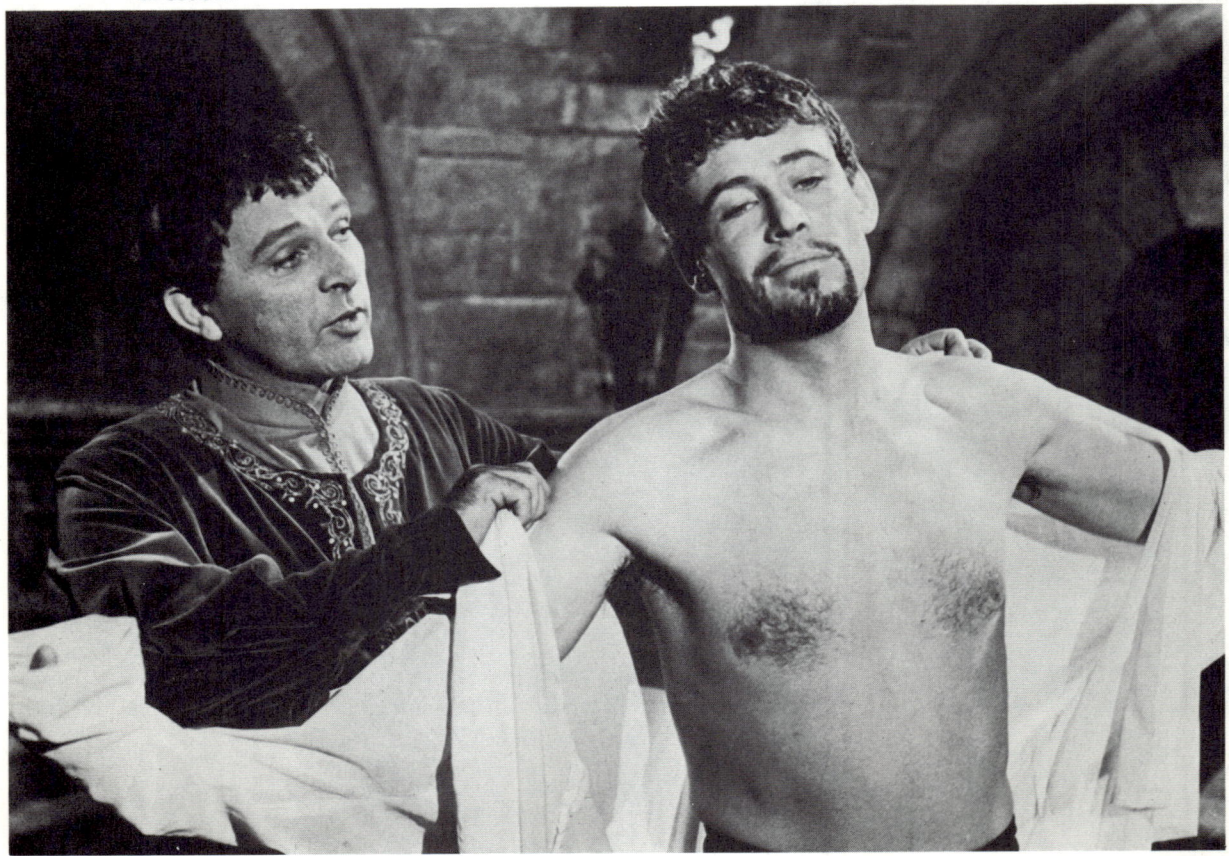

Richard Burton hands a film worker his cigarette as he prepares to shoot a bathing scene in *Cleopatra*.

George Sanders enjoys a glass of wine while relaxing in the tub in *The Best House in London*.

John Wayne seems to be ordering some soap for Robert Mitchum, in the tub, in this scene from *El Dorado*.

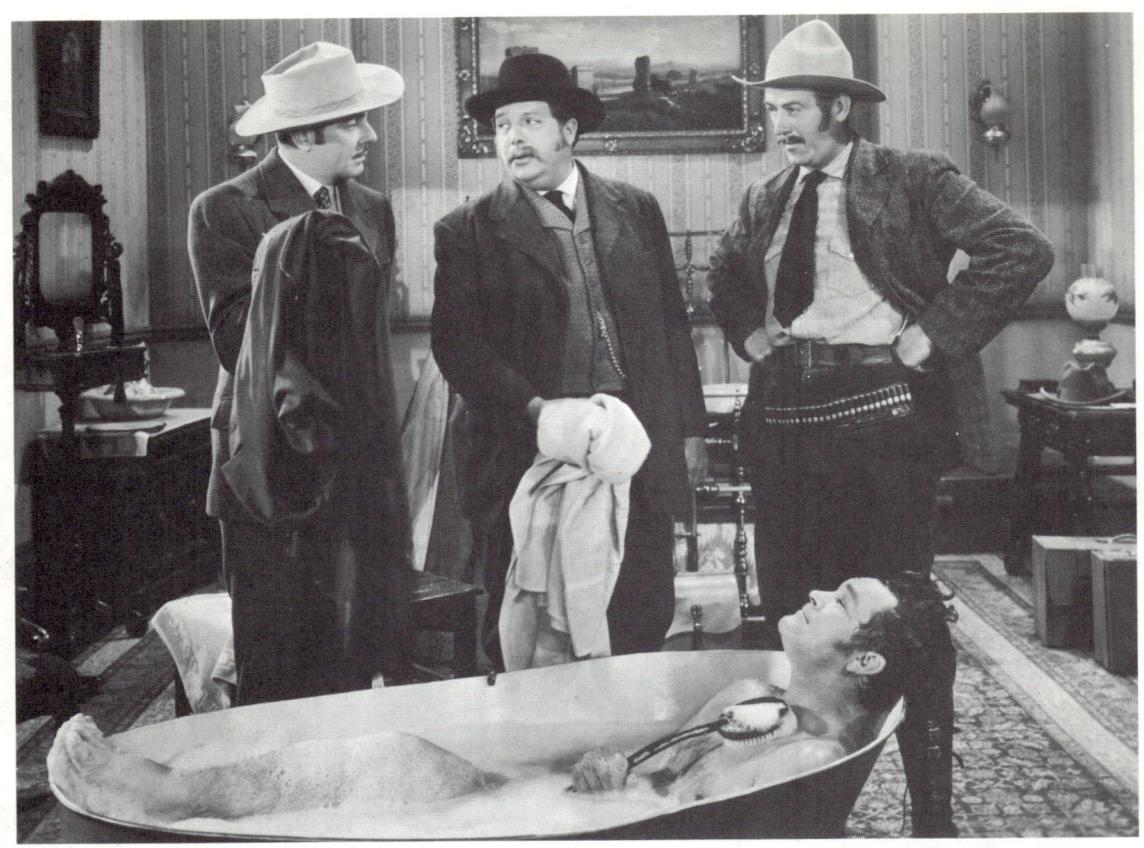
Guinn "Bib Boy" Williams scrubs himself in the *Silver Queen*, starring George Brent (left). Cy Kendall is in center, Roy Bancroft at right.

Bing Crosby sings a bathtub duet with Shirley Ross while she's in Paris and he's 1000 miles away in the Balkans. Edward Everett Horton interrupts the duet.

Eddie Bracken sits on a block of ice under a shower in *Out of this World*, a Paramount Picture with Cass Daley, Veronica Lake and Diana Lynn.

Gary Cooper's long legs stretch out in the tub in Cecil B. DeMille's *The Story of Dr. Wassell*. Laraine Day and Barbara Britton co-starred in the film.

A 1941 publicity shot by Paramount Pictures shows Richard Arlen in *A Morning in the Life of a Bachelor*, cleaning his own tub, and making quite a production out of it.

Don Murray plays a bus driver in *Bus Stop,* adapted from a play by William Inge. Arthur O'Connell is with Murray.

Preston Foster (left) and Arthur Treacher relaxing in tubs in a 1938 Twentieth Century Fox release called *Up the River.* Tony Martin, Phyllis Brooks and Slim Summerville also starred in the film.

Sam Whiskey (Burt Reynolds) lands in the tub during a fight with the blacksmith over the town's only public bathing facility in *Sam Whiskey*. Co-starring were Angie Dickinson, Ossie Davis and Clint Walker.

Barry Sullivan (foreground) and Gene Barry, in a scene from a western, *Forty Guns*.

Here's John Wayne getting his ears clean under the shower in *Big Jake*.

William Holden grimaces as water pours on his head in *The Horse Soldiers,* a 1958 Columbia Pictures release.

In *Mr. Peabody and the Mermaid,* it occurs to Mr. Peabody (William Powell) that his mermaid isn't used to hot water, or bathtubs either, for that matter.

James Cagney slaps Gig Young under the shower in *Come Fill the Cup,* a Warner Brothers story of a newspaperman and his fight against gangsters.

Peter Sellers ponders for a moment during a scene from *The Party*.

Laurence Olivier (left) and John Gavin in a scene from the 1961 spectacular, *Spartacus*.

Kirk Douglas (left) has a big laugh with Henry Fonda in *There Was a Crooked Man*. Hume Cronyn and Burgess Meredith also appear in the movie.

Robert Taylor relaxes in an ancient tub after a swashbuckling conflict with French warriors. Here, he discusses his latest combat with the Scottish ambassador, played by Moultrie Kelsall. The scene is from *Quentin Durward*. Kay Kendall and Robert Morley also starred.

Montgomery Clift is about to get a bucketful of water thrown on him in a scene from *Raintree County*.

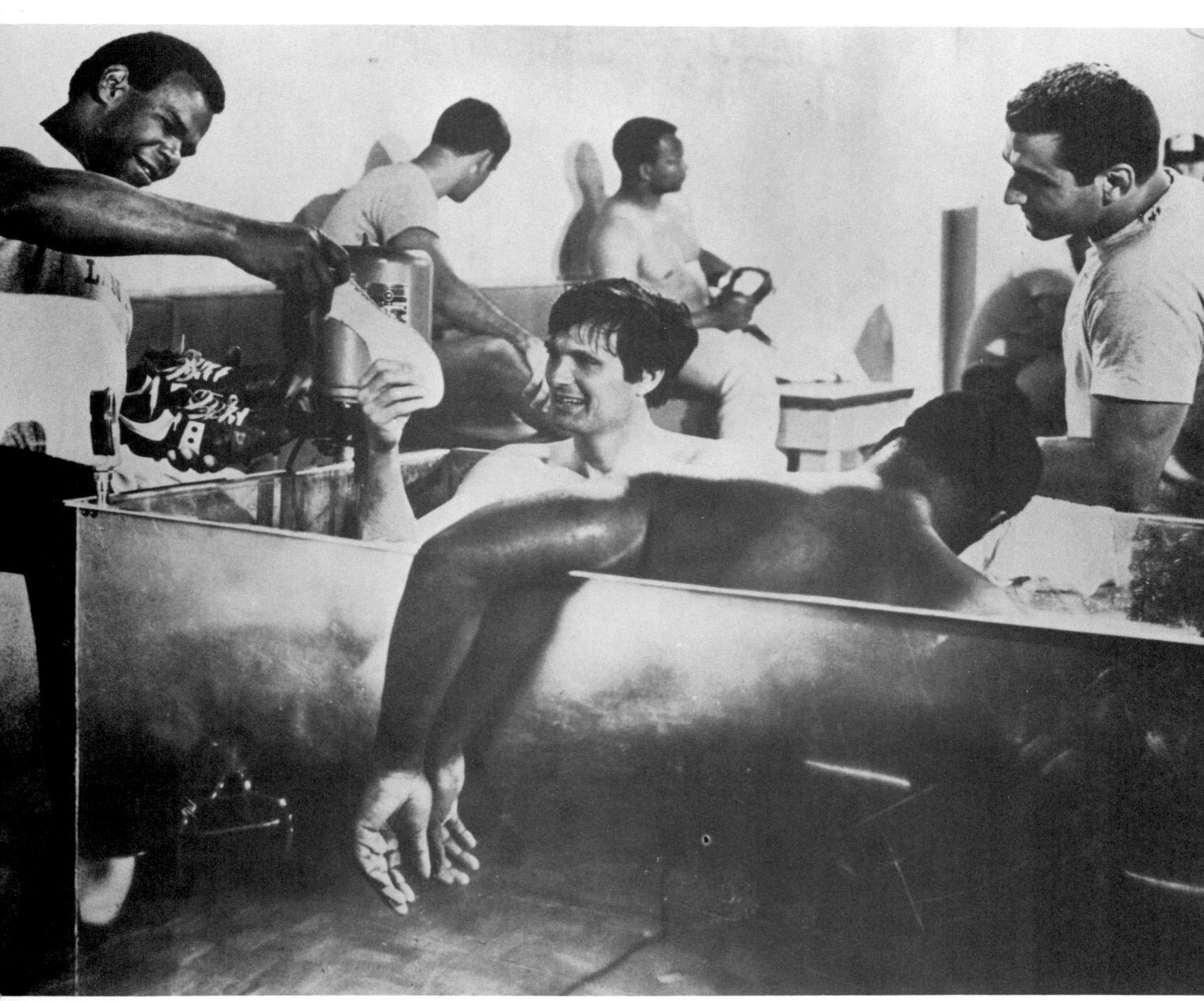
Alan Alda, star of the popular television series *Mash*, in a scene from *Paper Lion*, a movie about pro football.

The handsome physique of Guy Madison was used for publicizing the actor when he was an upcoming star in the 1940s.

In the film, *The Sting*, Paul Newman emerges from a tub after sobering up. Robert Redford waits patiently to talk to him.

Stephen McNally plays the role of a sports empire magnate who is mysteriously murdered while taking a whirlpool bath in *The Slave Trade*. This was a segment of MGM-TV's *Hawkins,* an early 1974 series.

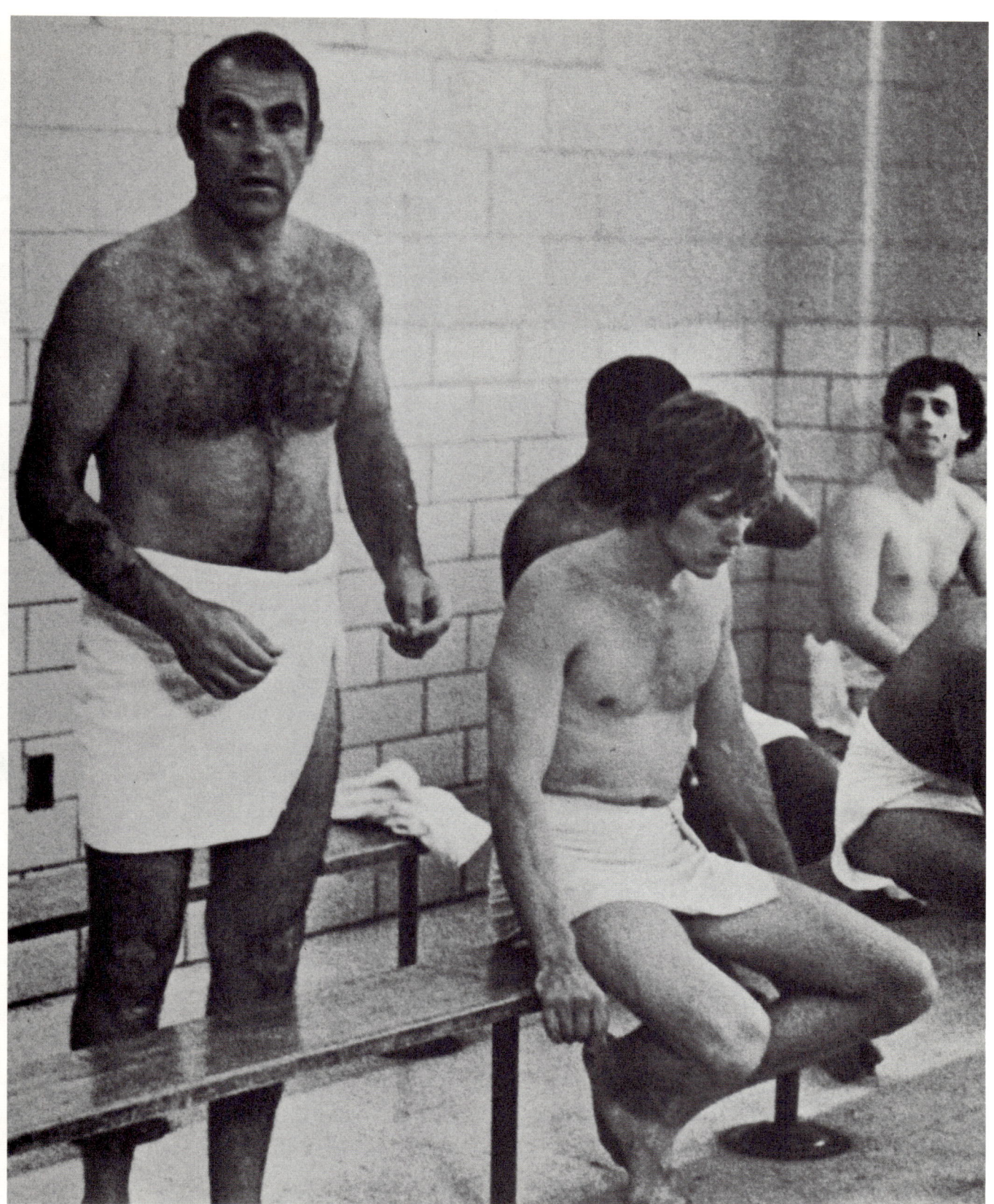
Sean Connery takes a steambath in *The Anderson Tapes,* based on the best-selling novel by Lawrence Sanders. Also featured in the film were Dyan Cannon, Martin Balsam and Alan King.

J. Edward McKinley tries to keep his cigar lit during the wild bubble bath scene in the Peter Sellers' movie, *The Party*.

Harry Dean Stanton is put to bed in a bathtub in this scene from *Where the Lilies Bloom,* a 1974 United Artists release.

Leo Gorcey (left) observes a friend getting a jungle-style shower in *Jungle Gents.*

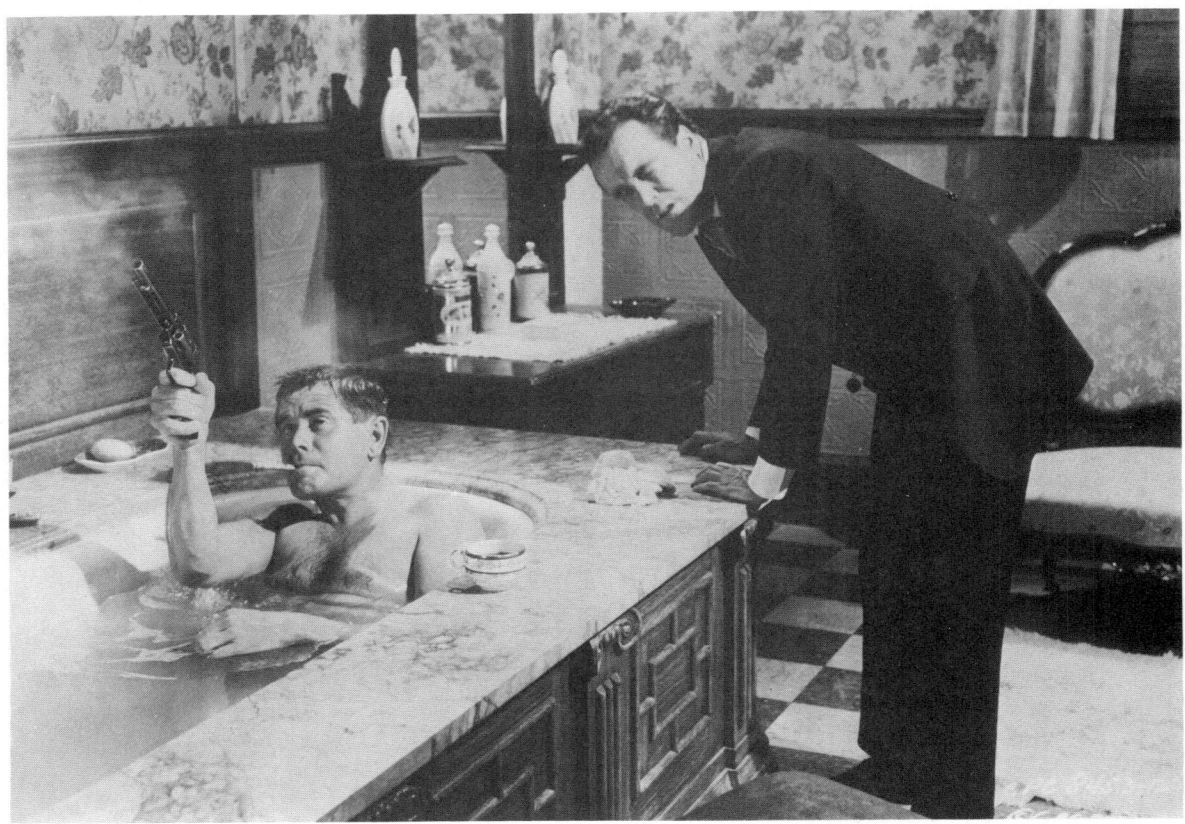
Glenn Ford fires his six-shooter while Jack Lemmon appears annoyed by the noise in *Cowboy,* a Columbia Pictures release.

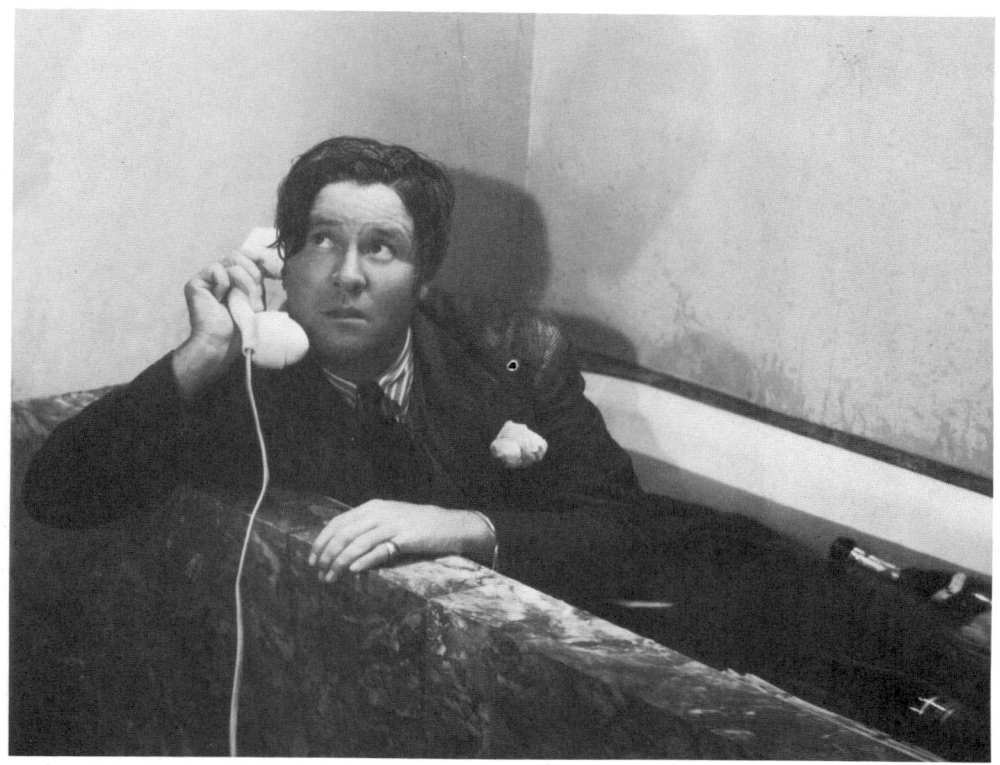

Jack Oakie, in a tub with champagne and wine bottles, takes a telephone call in *Annabel Takes a Tour*.

Victor Moore, at age 70 in 1946, tries to prove he can hold his own with Hollywood glamour queens by donning swimming trunks and slipping into a bubble bath in a beautiful marble tub in *It Happened on Fifth Avenue*.

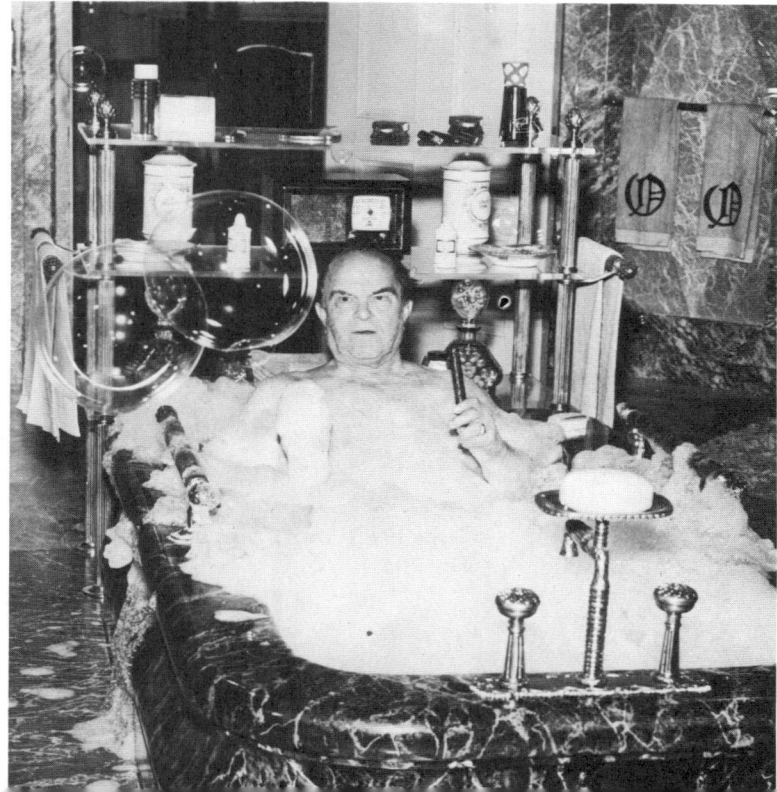

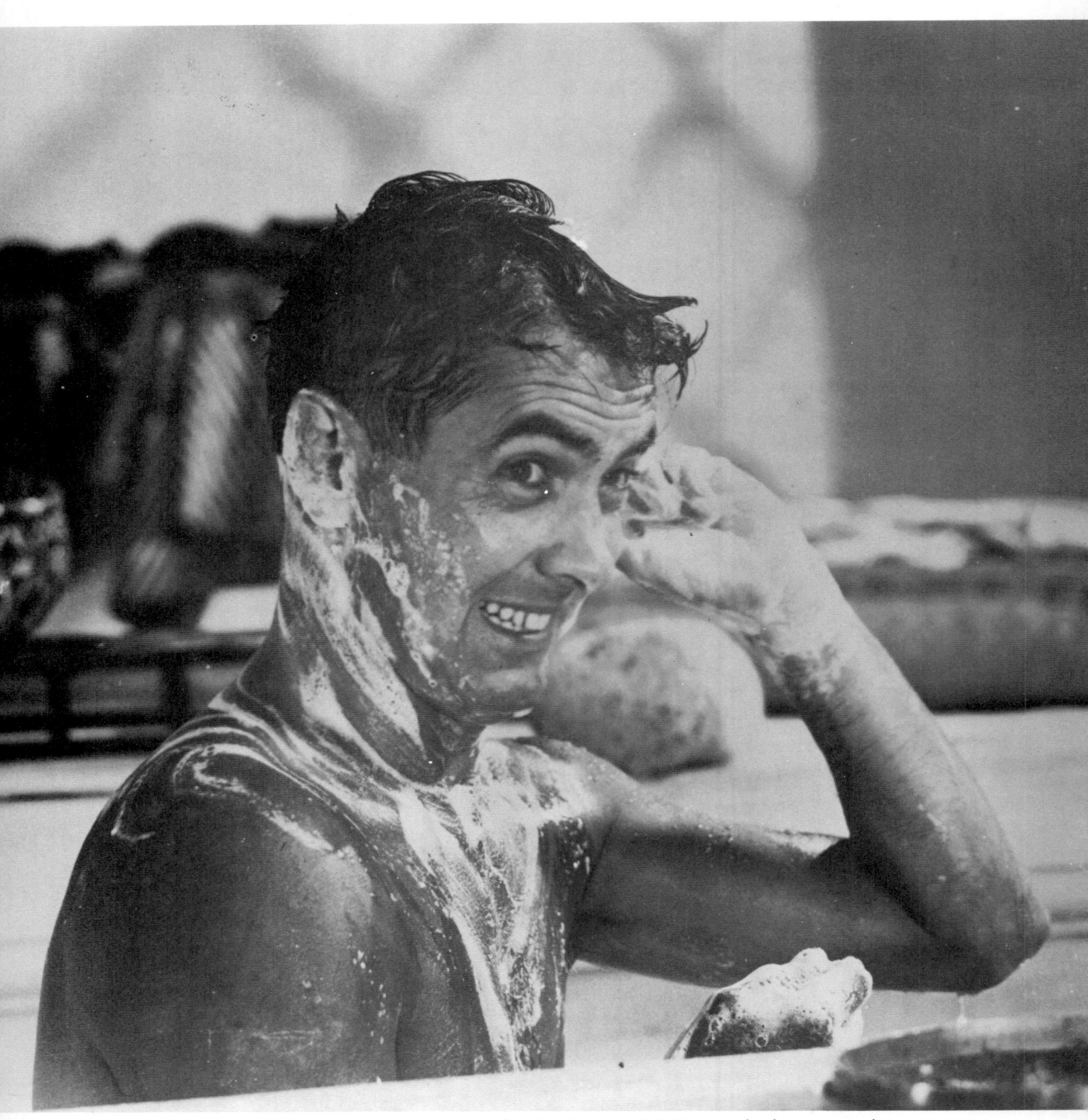
Tyrone Power, handsome actor of the 1940s and 1950s, in a bathing scene from a 20th Century Fox production, *The Black Rose*.

3
Male and Female Stars Together

In *Love in the Afternoon,* Gary Cooper takes his first film bath. Six beautiful Japanese Geisha girls help him.

Tuesday Weld played this scene in *The Cincinnati Kid* with her clothes on, while Steve McQueen was nude, somewhat of a reversal of the usual order in films. Also in the cast were Joan Blondell, Rip Torn and Jeff Corey.

James Bond, here played by Sean Connery, always has some interesting scenes with pretty girls. This one is from *You Only Live Twice*.

Rock Hudson and Julie Andrews in Paramount Pictures' *Darling Lili,* a 1968 release.

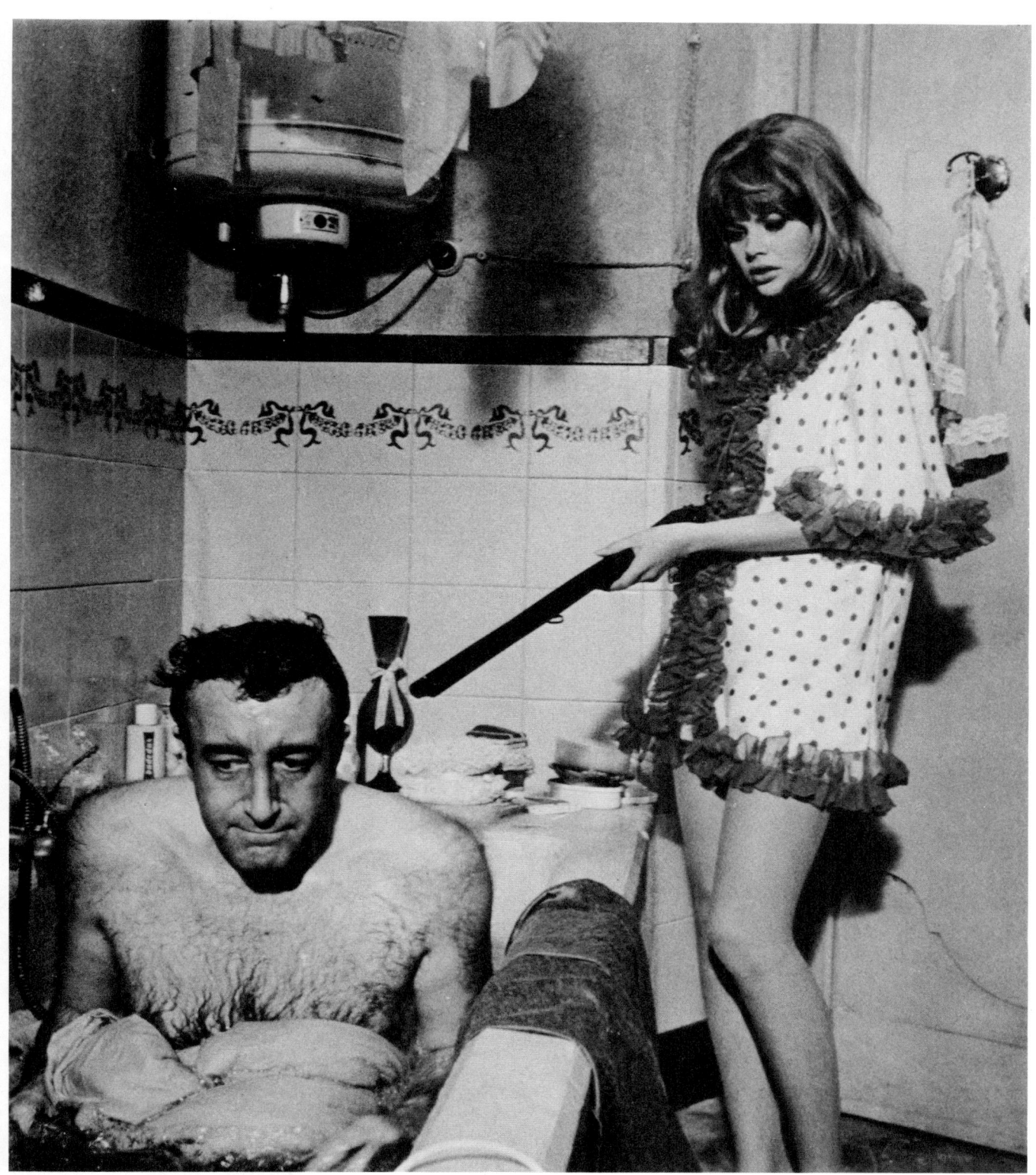
Peter Sellers and Britt Ekland are shown in Warner Brothers' *The Bobo*.

Peter Sellers invites Leigh Taylor-Young into his bathroom in *I Love You, Alice B. Toklas*. Jo Van Fleet was a co-star.

Dean Martin and Shirley MacLaine keep their clothes on for this scene from *All in a Night's Work*.

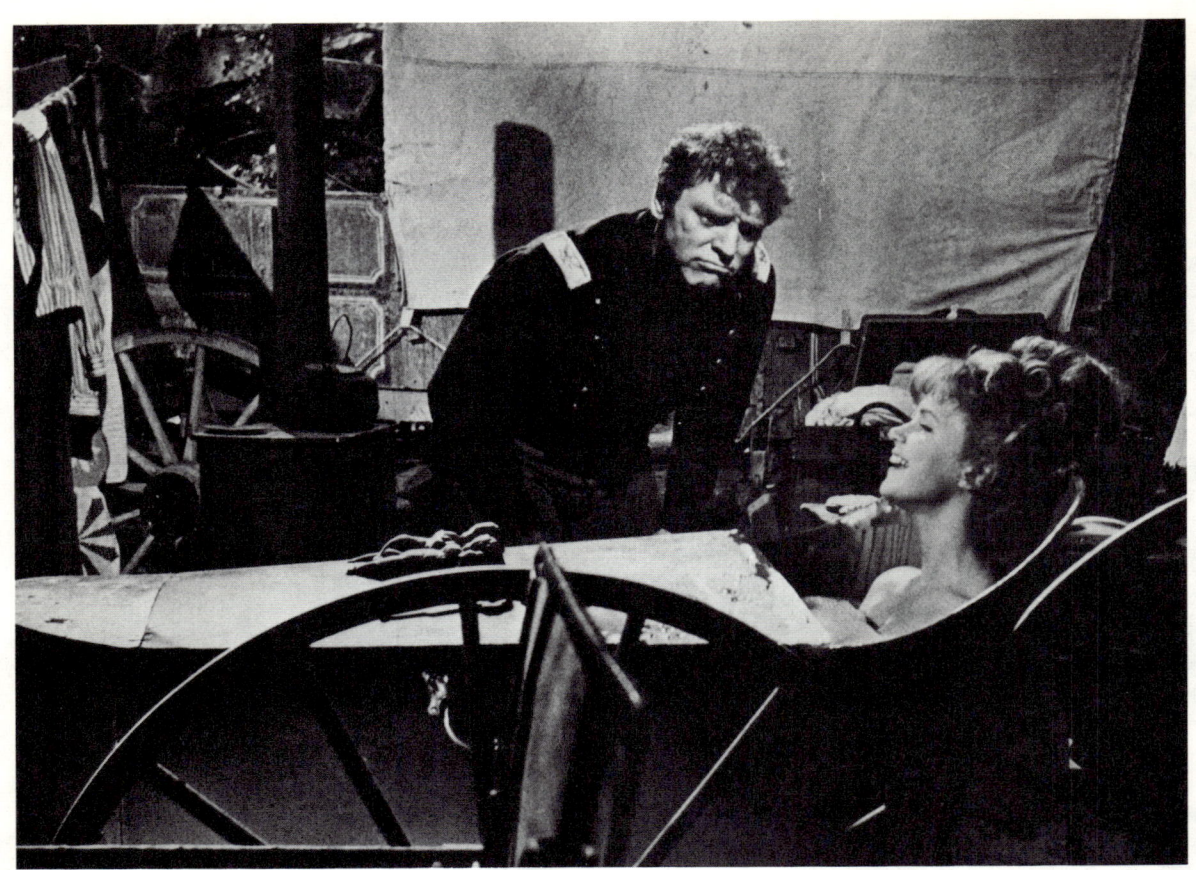

Burt Lancaster and Lee Remick take turns bathing in *The Hallelujah Trail*. Jim Hutton and Pamela Tiffin also starred in this John Sturges movie.

Ava Gardner asks Clark Gable for her robe as she steps from under an outdoor shower in this jungle scene from *Mogambo*, filmed in Africa. The film was directed by John Ford and produced by Sam Zimbalist.

Henry Fonda keeps his hat on as he bathes before three beauties in *Welcome to Hard Times*.

Dustin Hoffman is given a bath by a friend, Mrs. Pendrake, played by Faye Dunaway in *Little Big Man*. Martin Balsam co-starred.

Sharon Tate and Roman Polanski in a scene from *The Fearless Vampire Killers or Pardon Me, But Your Teeth Are in My Neck*, a Martin Ransohoff-Roman Polanski production.

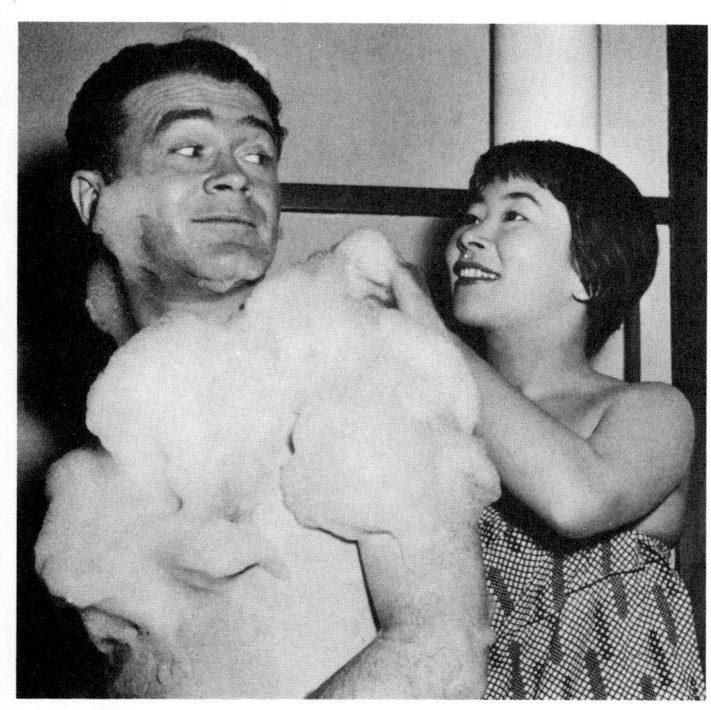

(Left) Comedian Red Buttons receives help as he prepares for a bath in *Sayonara,* a movie in which he plays an American airman married to a Japanese girl.

(Below) Robert Wagner, in the tub with his clothes on, shares the soap suds with Capucine in *Pink Panther,* while Peter Sellers surveys the situation.

Glynis Johns prepares for a sudsy sequence as special effects men stir up bubbles. Co-star Robert Wagner and director Ron Winston (with glasses) discuss the action in Universal's *don't just STAND there*. Barbara Rhoades also starred in the film.

Mary Tyler Moore (left), Robert Wagner and an immersed Barbara Rhoades in a scene from *don't just STAND there*.

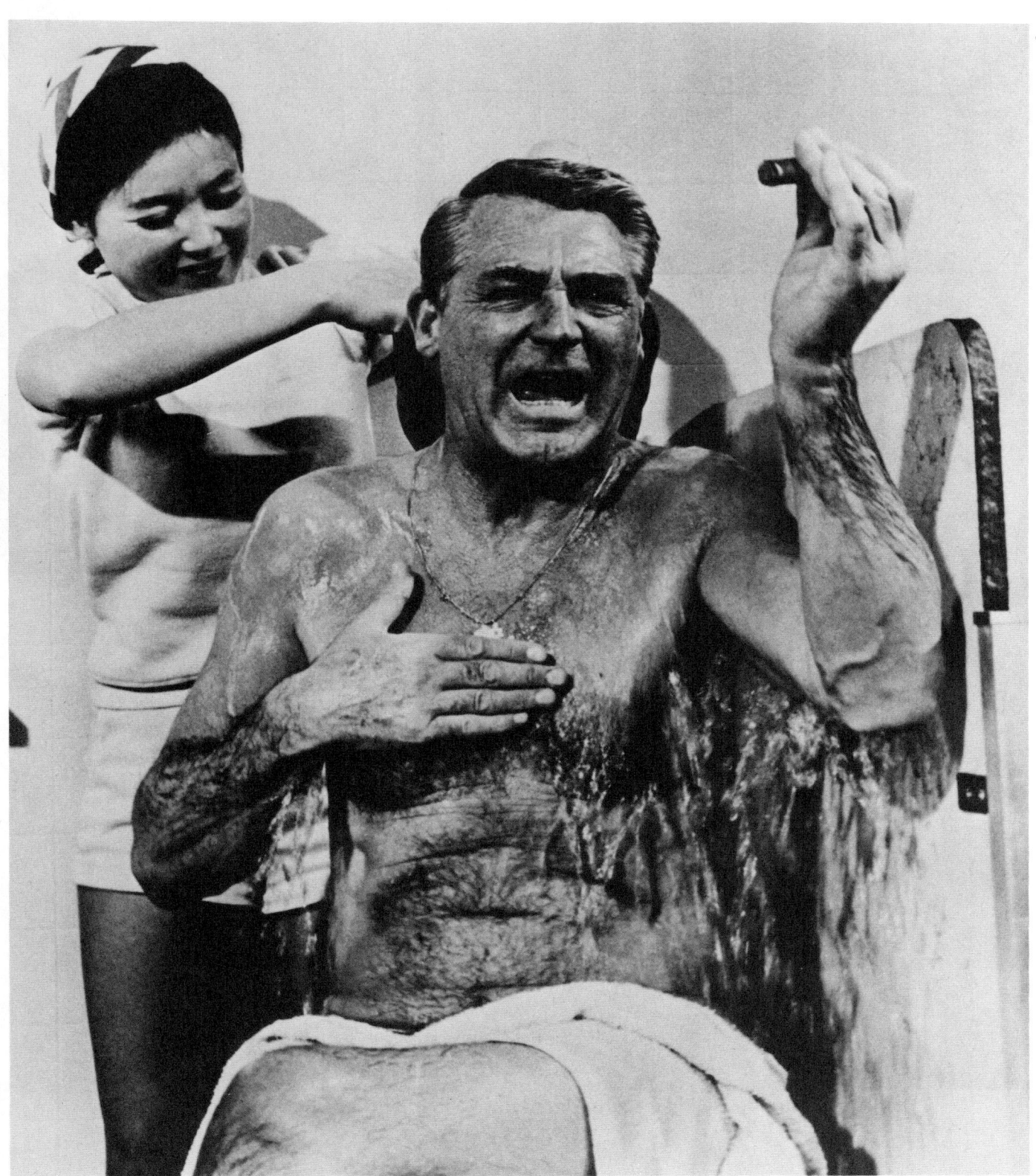
Cary Grant feels the shock of cold water in this scene from *Walk, Don't Run*.

Tony Curtis, dressed like a girl, with Marilyn Monroe in a bathing scene from *Some Like It Hot*.

A wild soap bubble bath scene takes place in *The Party*, a 1968 film co-starring Peter Sellers (at far left).

Jack Lemmon receives a visit from Juliet Mills in this bathing scene from *Avanti*.

Robert Vaughn greets Evon Craig with a kiss in *One Spy Too Many*, a 1966 MGM release of an Arena Production.

Bob Hope covers up bashfully in *Road to Hong Kong,* one of his several "road" films.

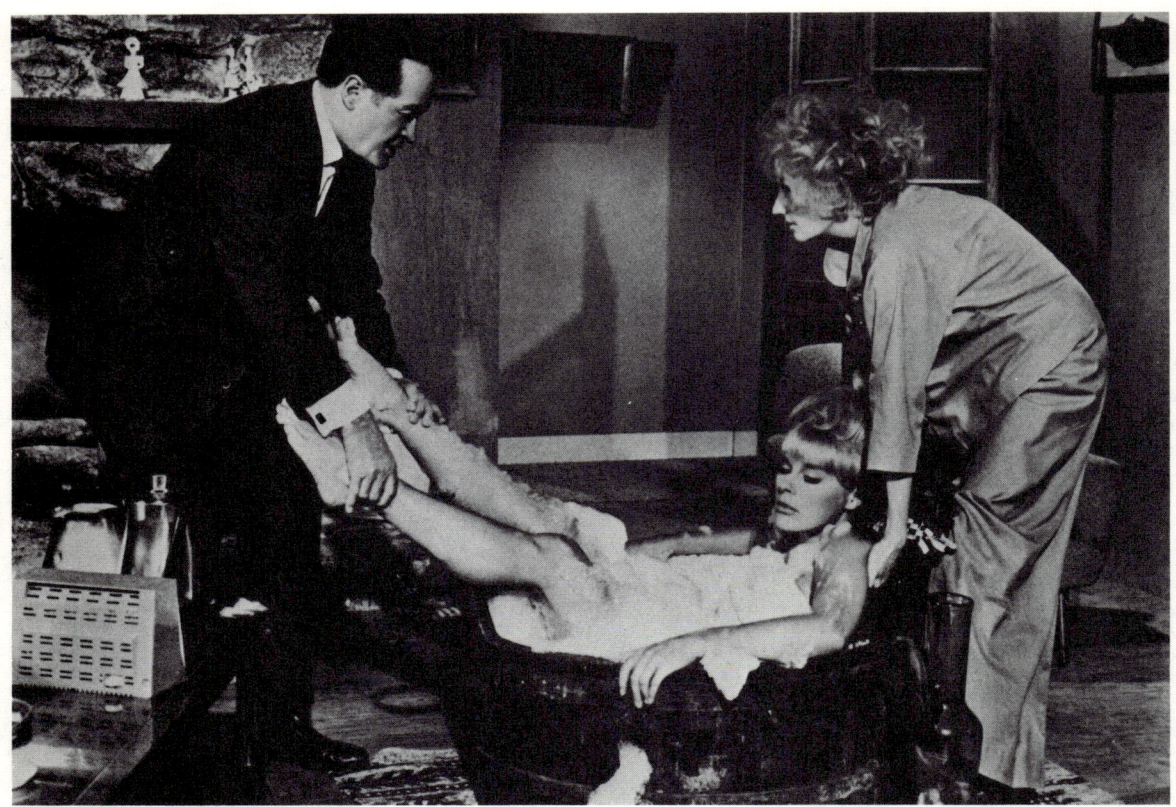
Bob Hope and Phyllis Diller help Elke Sommer out of a tub in *Boy, Did I Get a Wrong Number.*

Gina Lollobrigida's luxurious bath is interrupted by a visit from Frank Sinatra in *Never So Few.*

Don Stroud receives some assistance with his bath from Shelley Winters in *Bloody Mama,* based on the story of gang leader Ma Barker, a notorious criminal of the 1930s.

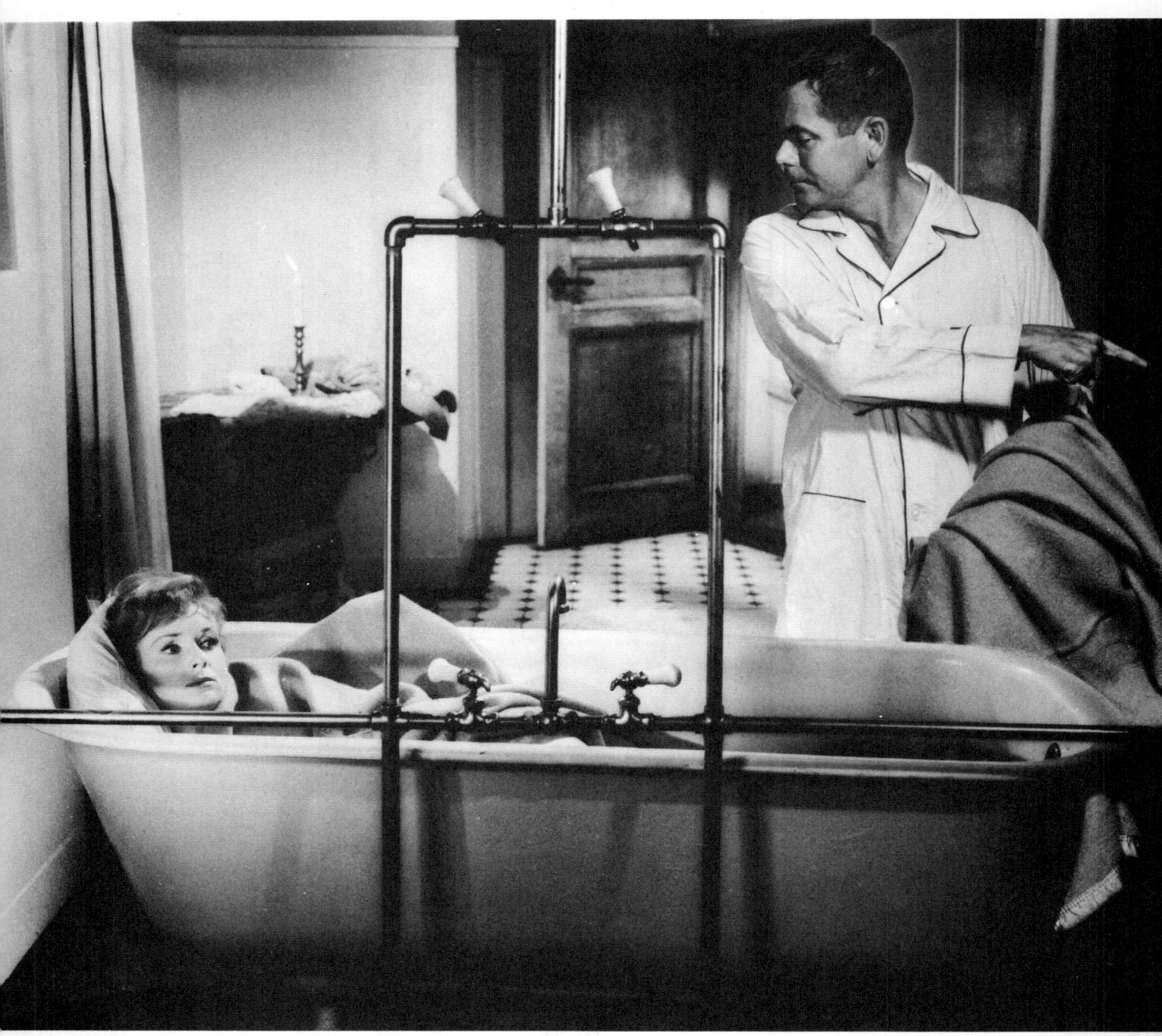

Debbie Reynolds and Glenn Ford select a most unusual place for patching up a marital spat in *It Started With a Kiss*. Also appearing in the movie were Eva Gabor, Gustavo Rojo and Fred Clair.

Wendy Hiller helps Trevor Howard with his bath, while Dean Stockwell is busy studying in *Sons and Lovers*.

Speaking of unusual bathtubs! Benita Hume talks things over while Adolph Menjou reads a trade magazine.

Clark Gable complains to Jean Harlow, "That's our drinking water," when he comes upon her taking a hot bath in this rare photo from *Red Dust,* a 1932 movie.

Diana Lynn's small tub doesn't offer enough space for a friend in a deep-sea diving suit in *My Friend Irma.*

4
The Comics

A rare photograph showing a Fatty Arbuckle routine. This scene by the famous comedian of the 1920s is from a Mack Sennett film entitled *Mad, Mad . . . World.*

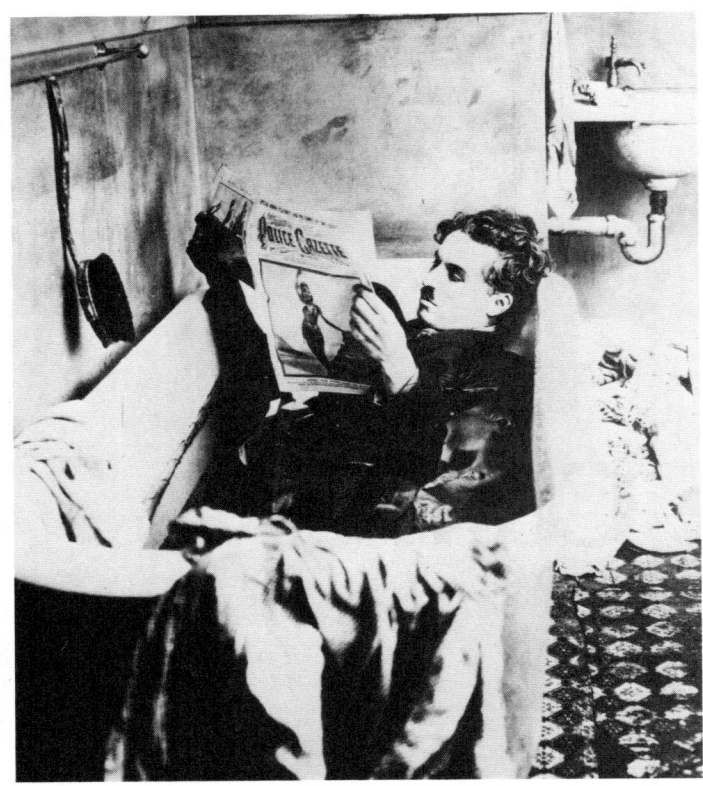

Charlie Chaplin, popular silent screen comedian, reads the Police Gazette in a tub filled with water while wearing his clothes, in the 1922 film, *Pay Day*.

Harold Lloyd, in this 1938 scene from *Professor, Beware!* is discovered as a stowaway in a honeymoon trailer by the newlyweds themselves, played by Mary Lou Lender and Sterling Holloway.

In *Forever and a Day*, Sir Cedric Hardwicke (left) and Buster Keaton are directed by Jessie Matthews as they install an iron bath.

Buster Keaton, a comedian of the 1920s, is taking both a bath and a shower in one of his many comedy routines.

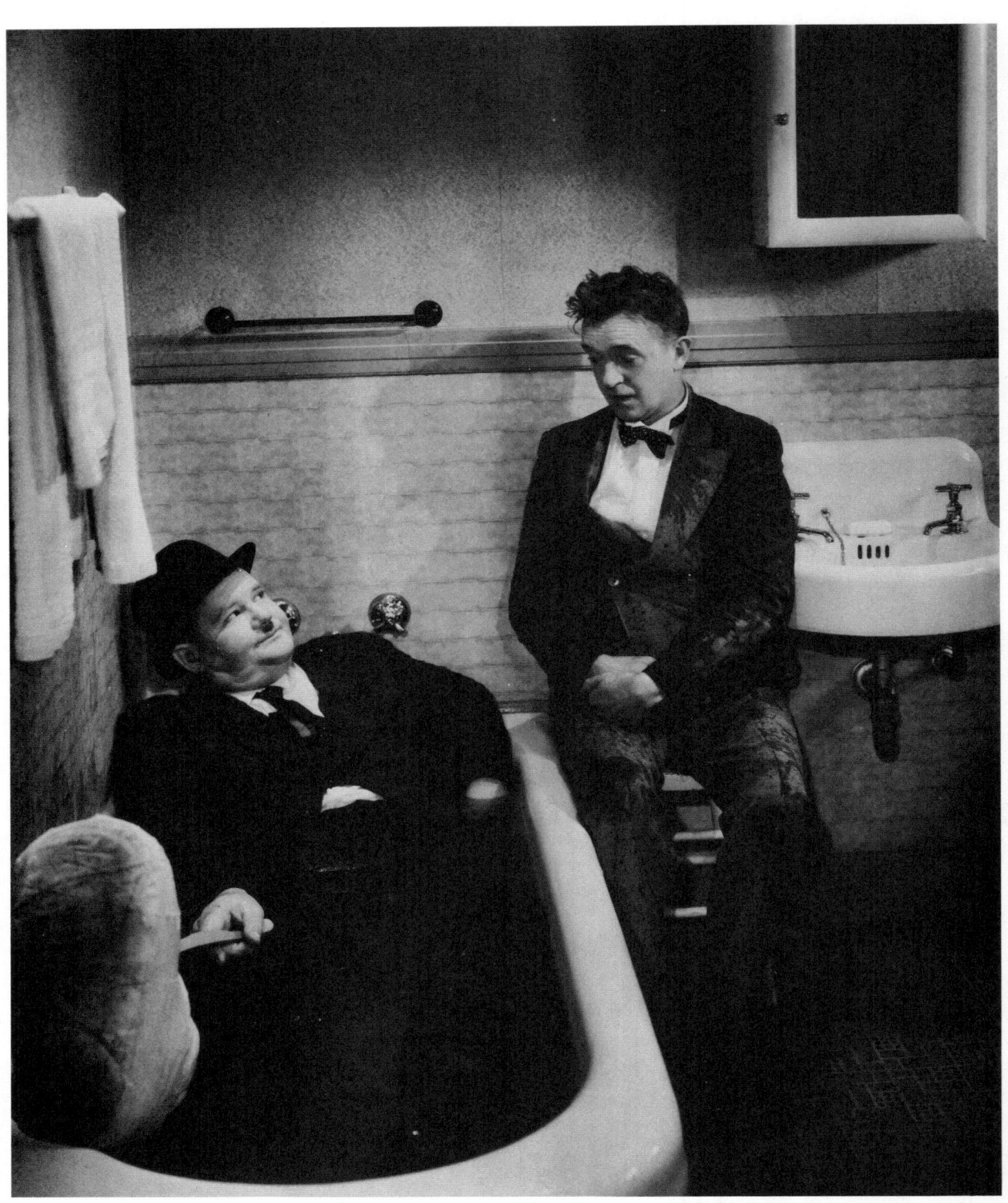
Laurel and Hardy find themselves in a difficult situation in this bathtub scene from one of their many hilarious films.

(Above) Laurel and Hardy played many a bathing scene for laughs in their popular comedies of the 1930s. (Below) Laurel and Hardy, in *Bonnie Scotland,* salute Jimmy Finlayson.

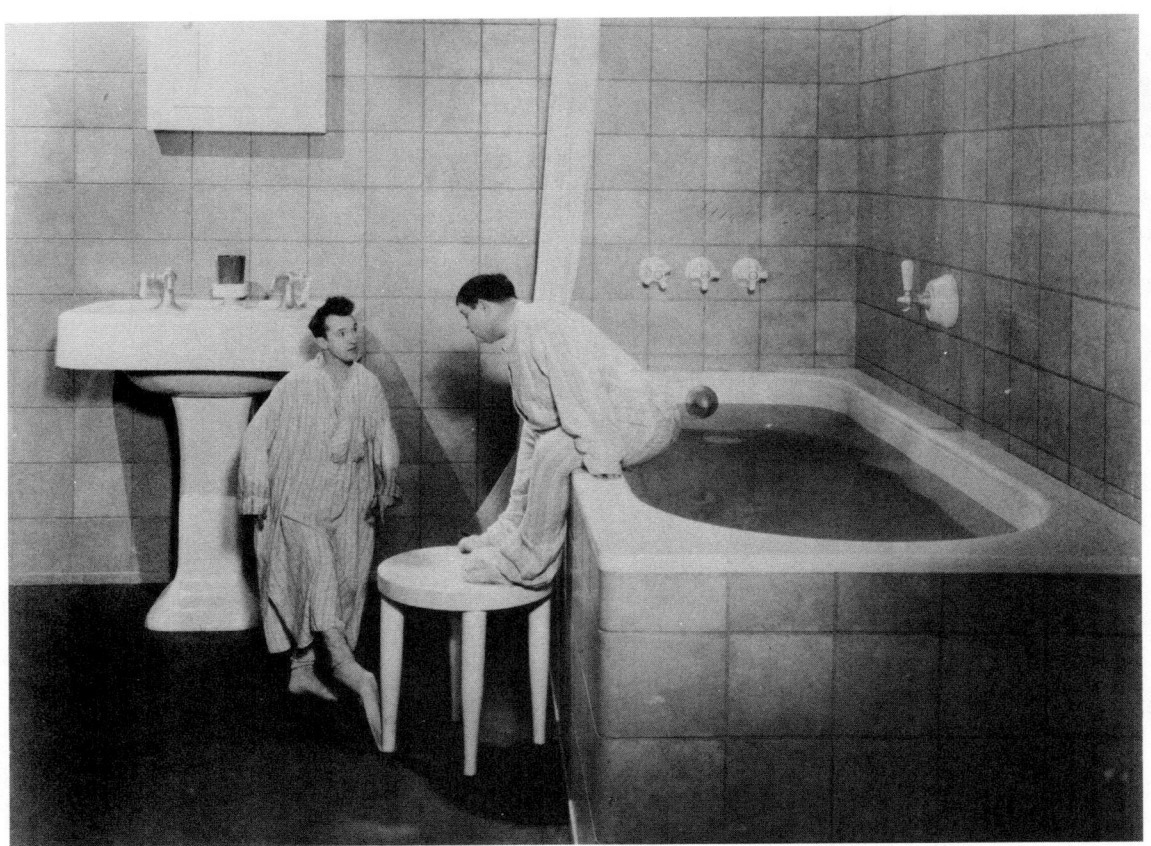
Laurel and Hardy in one of their famous bathtub scenes from *Brats*.

Joe E. Brown opens his famous big mouth as he prepares for a steambath in *Hold Everything*, an early Warner Brothers production.

A rare photograph showing Bud Abbott and Lou Costello (right) confronted by a serious situation. This is a scene from *In Society*, a 1944 Universal production.

As usual, Bud Abbott and Lou Costello are in plenty of hot water. *Africa Screams*, the 1949 film from which this scene was taken, also featured Clyde Beatty and Frank Buck.

The Three Stooges, famous movie comedy team, use a bathtub for one of their mad routines.

Jack Benny drops in on Mary Martin in *Love Thy Neighbor,* a 1940 Paramount picture.

Groucho Marx, puffing furiously on his inevitable cigar, tests the temperature of the water with his big toe in *Double Dynamite*.

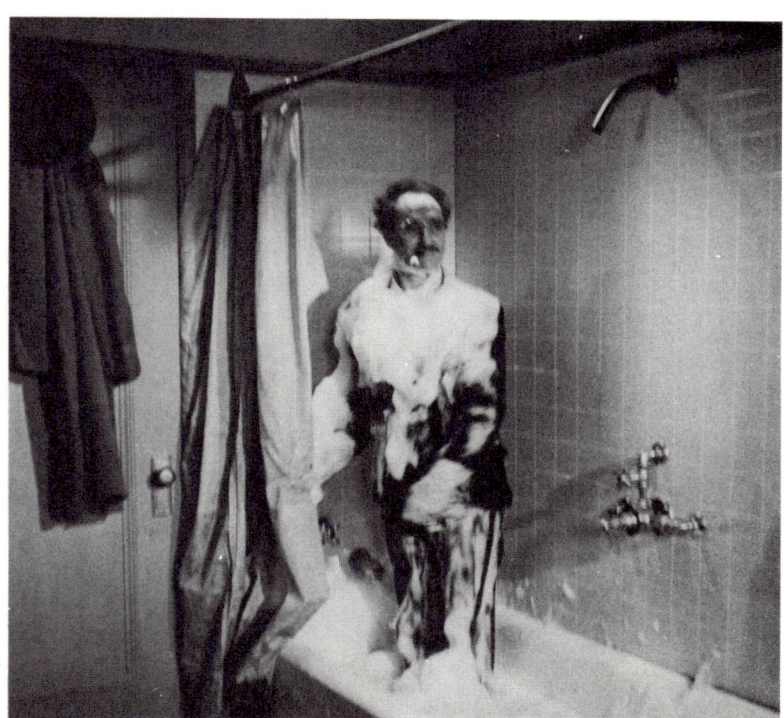

Taking a bath with his clothes on, Groucho Marx, still puffing on his cigar, gets so wet that his glasses shrink in this scene from *It's Only Money*. Also starring in the film: Frank Sinatra and Jane Russell.

Between scenes for *A Day At the Circus,* a 1939 MGM movie, Harpo Marx demonstrates how a guest in a midget's home would have to brush his teeth.

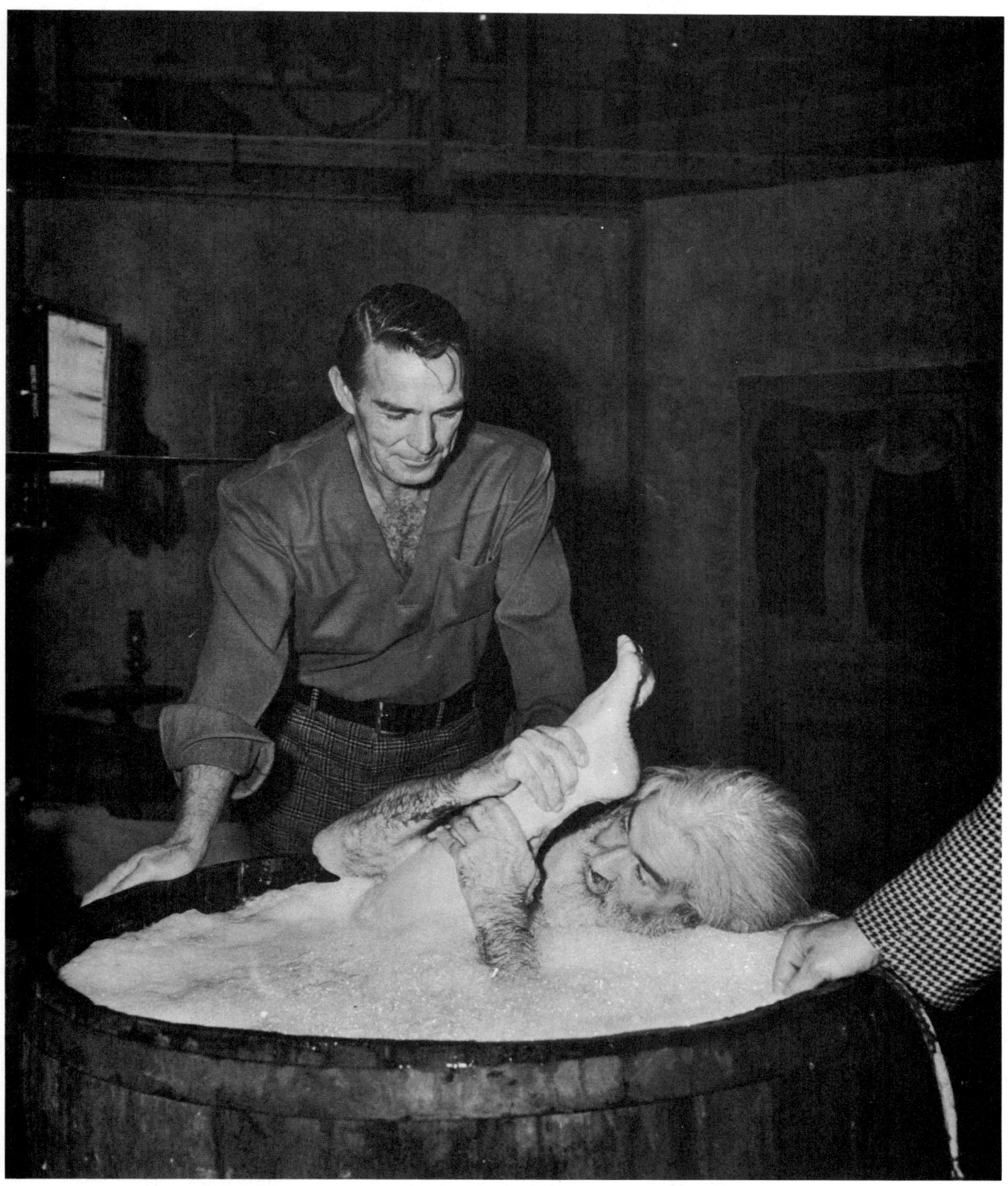

George "Gabby" Hayes, as the bewhiskered western comic, demonstrates to Randolph Scott that he's as limber as a twig in this scene from the Paramount film, *Albuquerque*.

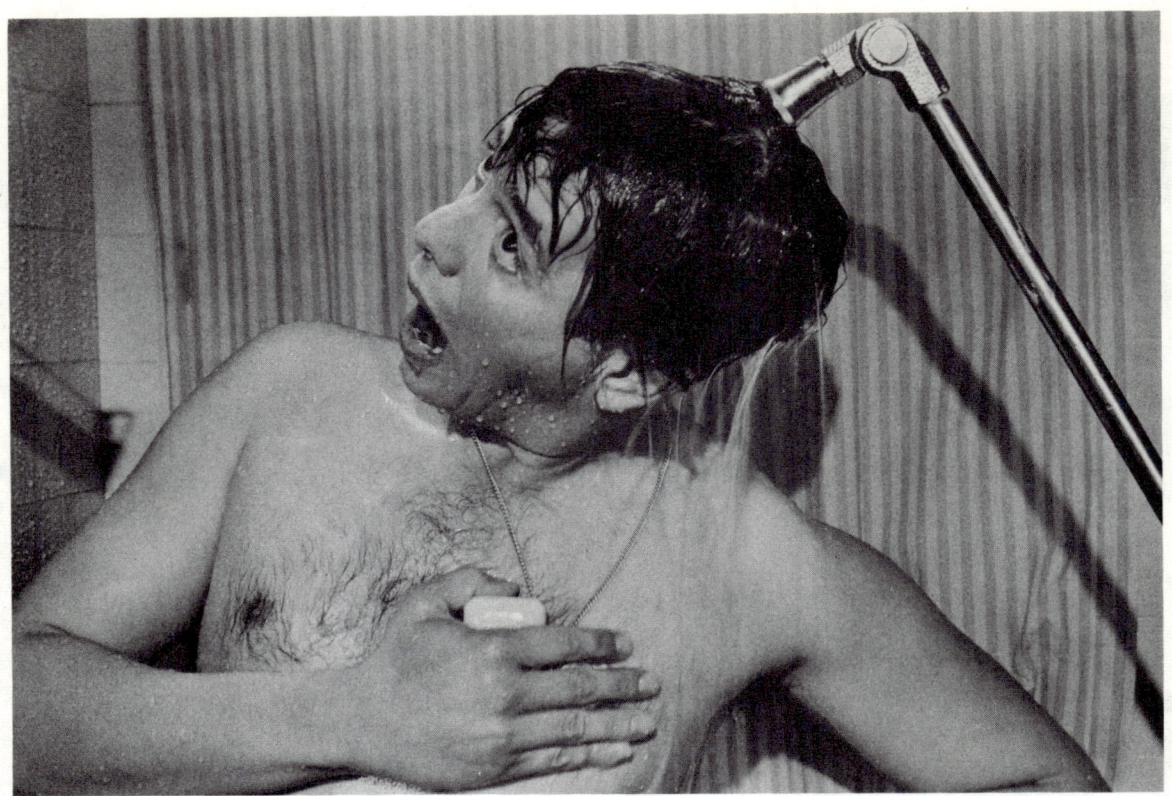

Desi Arnaz finds that a honeymoon on wheels can be a bumpy affair, especially when under a shower, in a 1953 MGM comedy, *Showered With Trouble,* with Lucille Ball.

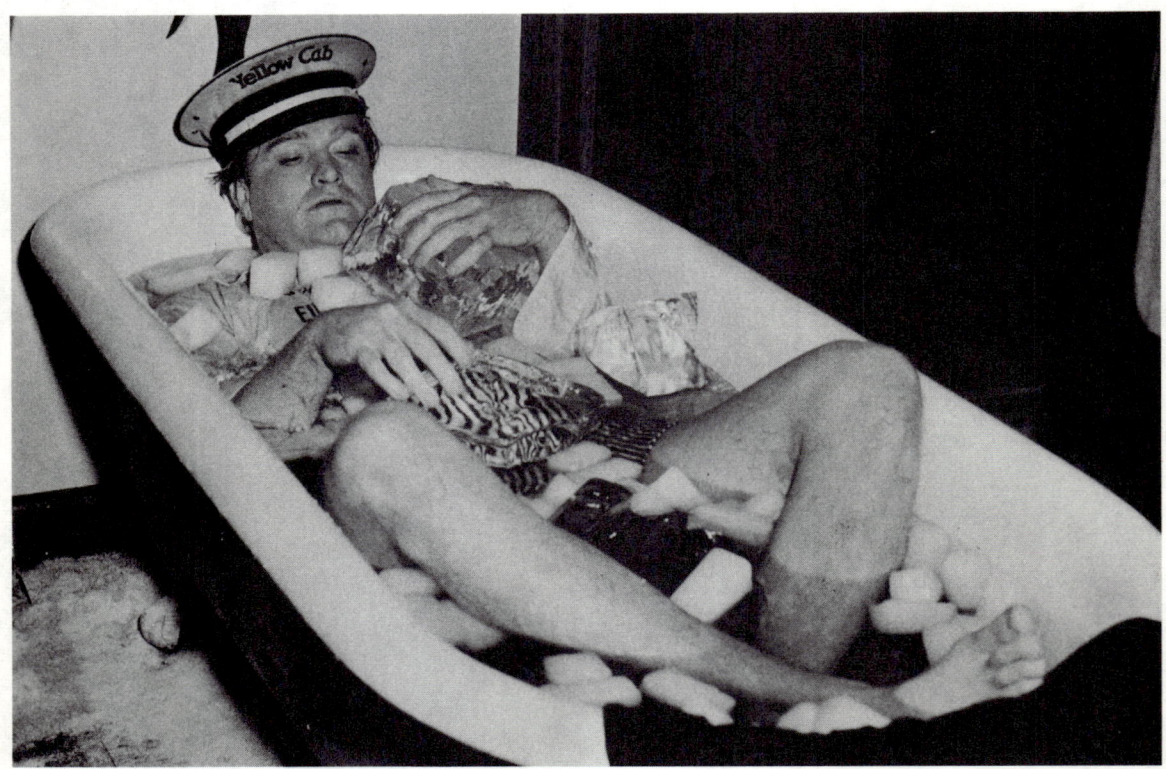

A sequence in the 1949 film, *Yellow Cab Man,* called for Red Skelton to be immersed in a tub of ice water as a shock treatment to help him recover from a car accident. Red spent four hours in the icy waters before the director was satisfied.

Bob Hope gets involved in a bathtub caper with Jack Kirkwood in *Fancy Pants,* a 1950 Paramount Picture release. Lucille Ball co-starred.

Bob Hope rushes into the room wrapped in a towel when he hears Jack Benny play a few bars from his theme song ("Thanks For the Memory") on *The Jack Benny Program,* a popular NBC television program for many seasons.

Bob Hope is caught hiding in the shower. William Bendix points a gun at him in *Star Spangled Rhythm,* an MCA-TV film.

W.C. Fields, the famous comic of the 1930s, in one of many bathing scenes in which he appeared over the years.

Jerry Lewis luxuriates, fully clothed, in a Roman bath during a comedy sketch from *The Jerry Lewis Show* on NBC-TV.

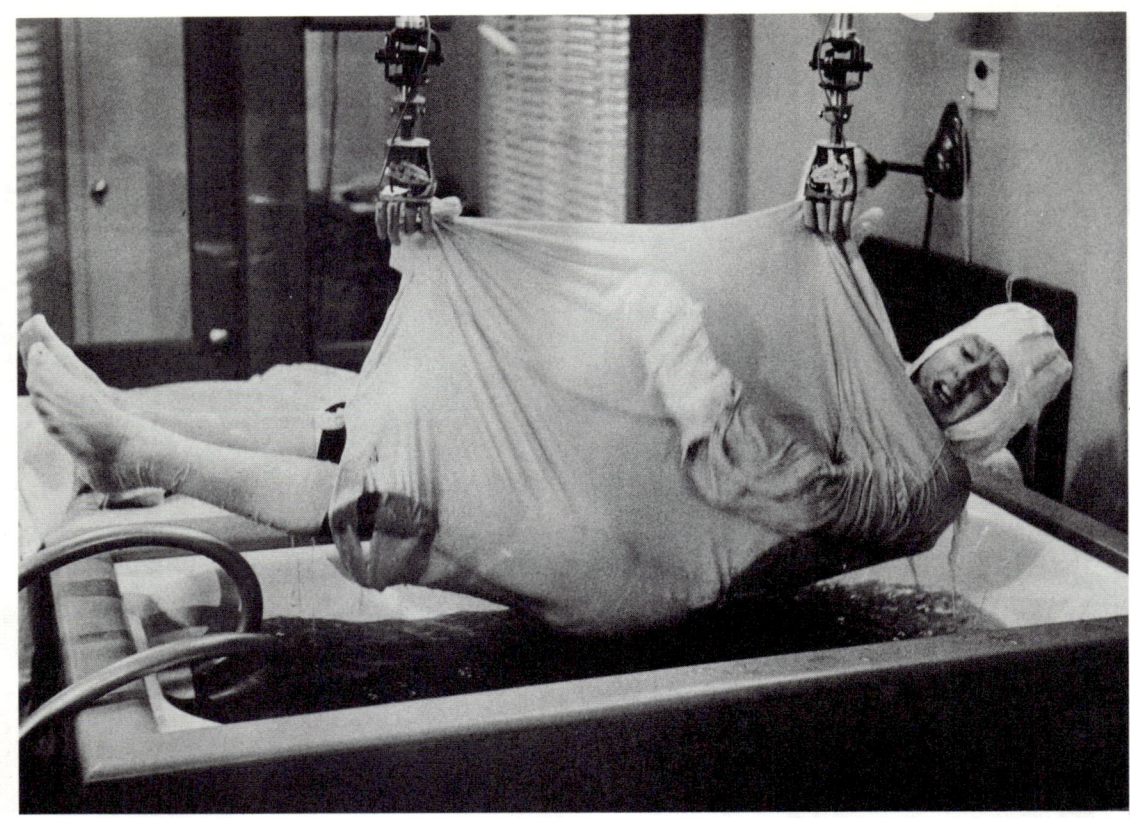

Young Mickey Rooney finds himself thoroughly bandaged in this scene as he is about to be immersed in a therapy bath.

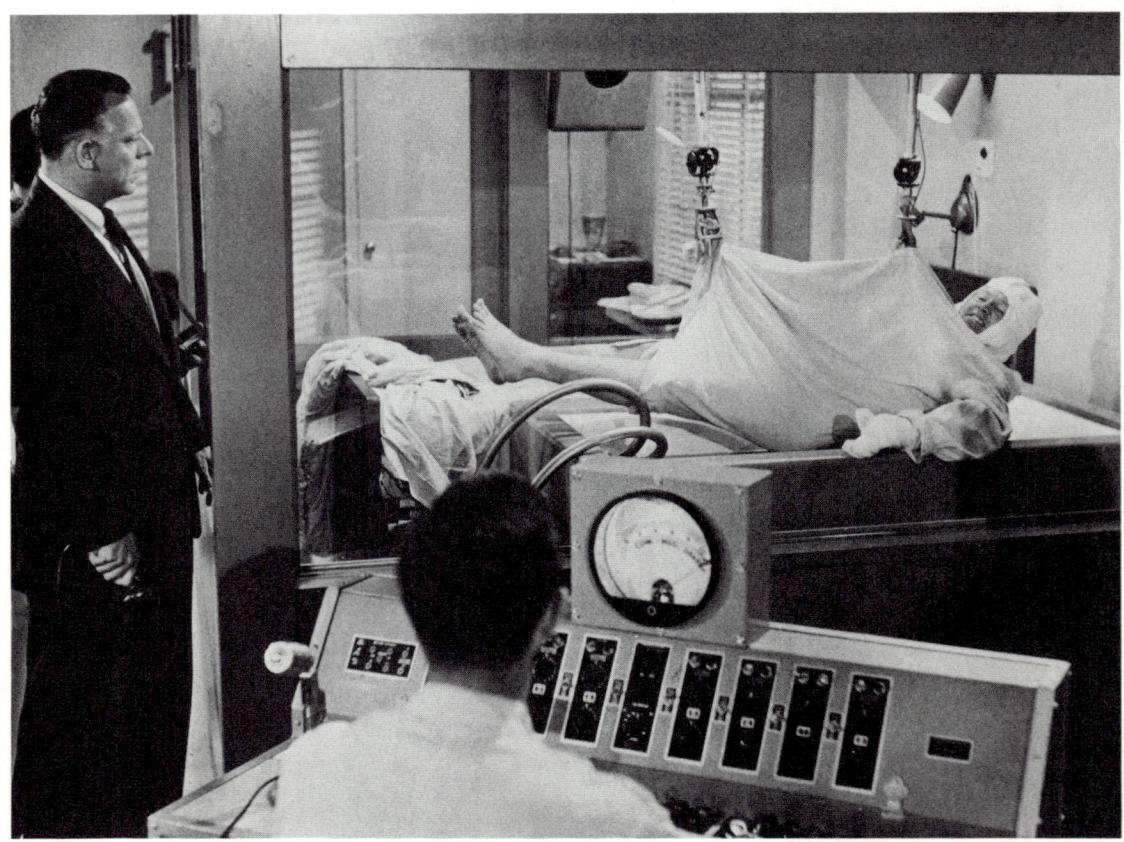

5
Children and Animals

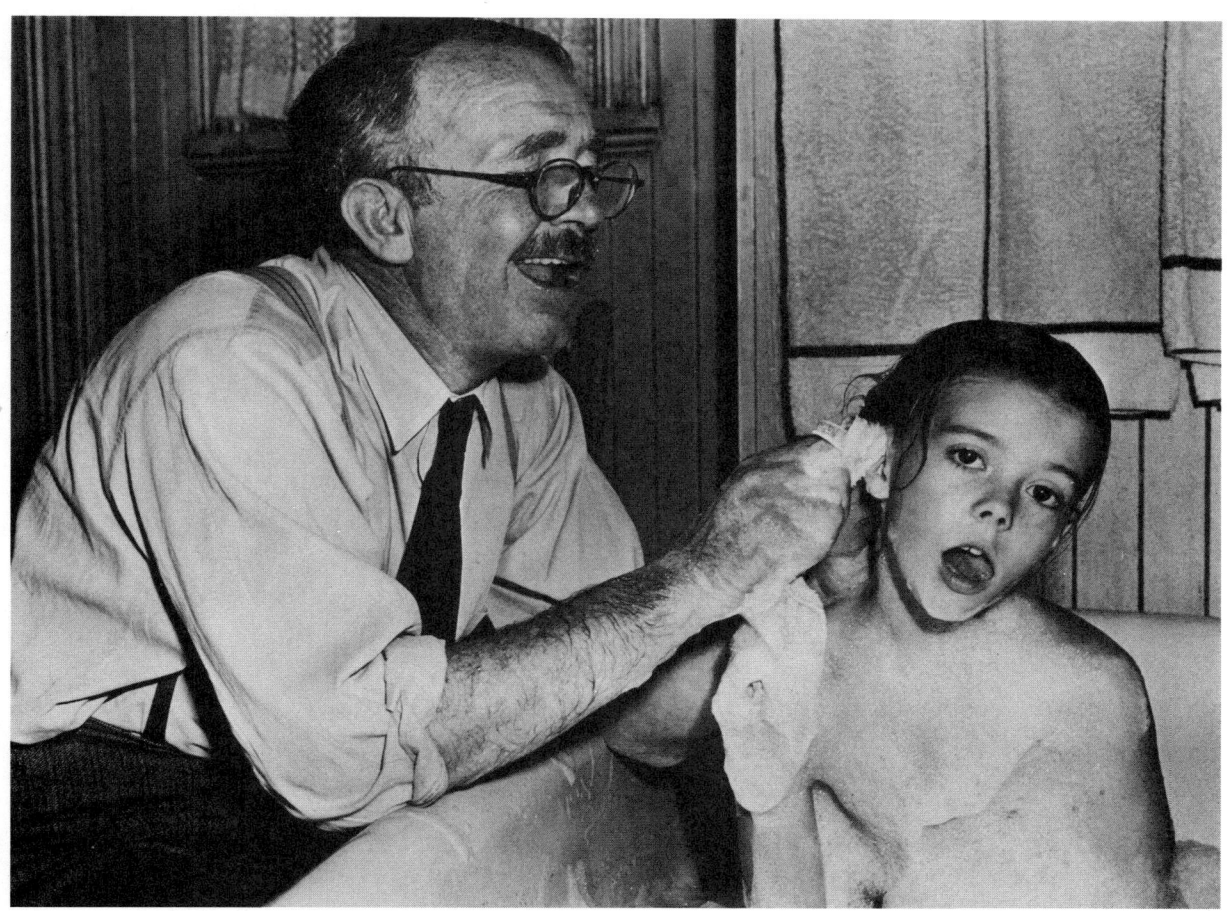

Natalie Wood, now Mrs. Robert Wagner, is shown bathing in one of her several films as a child actress.

This is not a movie scene. It's Rosalind Russell giving a bath to her then 3½-year-old son, Lance Brisson, at their home in Beverly Hills. At the time, she was co-starring with Melvyn Douglas in *The Guilt of Janet Ames*.

Bert Lahr gives some fatherly advice to Jimmy Boyd in *The Second Greatest Sex,* a 1955 Universal Pictures release.

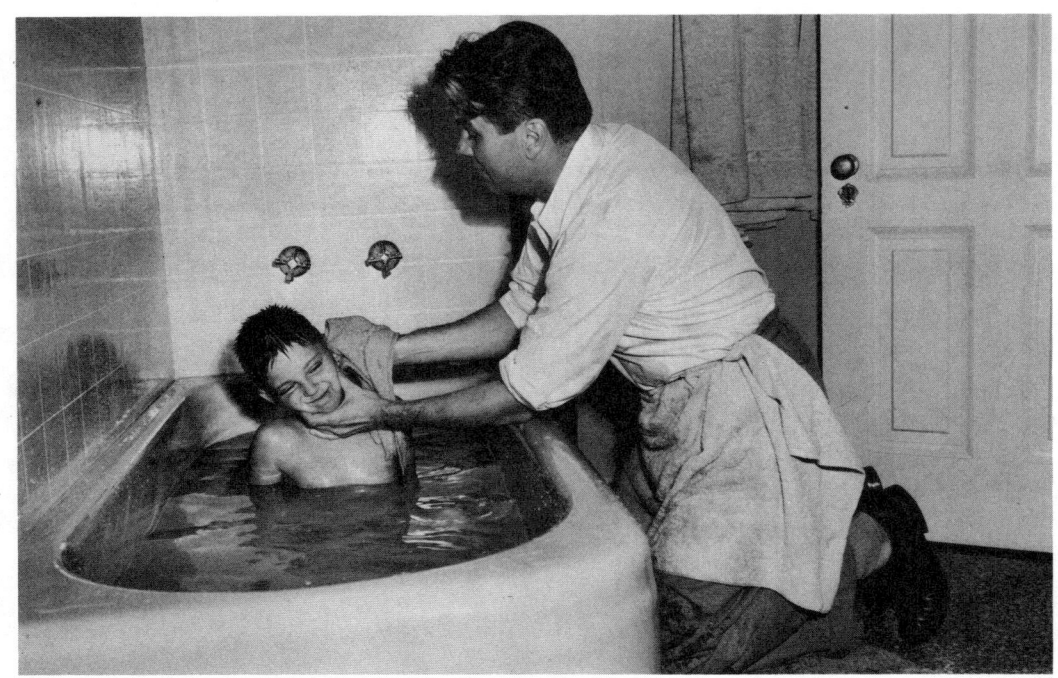

(Above) Kent Smith learns how to bathe eight-year-old Tommy Rettig in this scene from the 1951 Columbia release, *Paula*, which starred Loretta Young.

(Below) Mary Jane Saunders enjoys a bubble bath in the 1948 Paramount movie, *Sorrowful Jones*, starring Bob Hope and Lucille Ball.

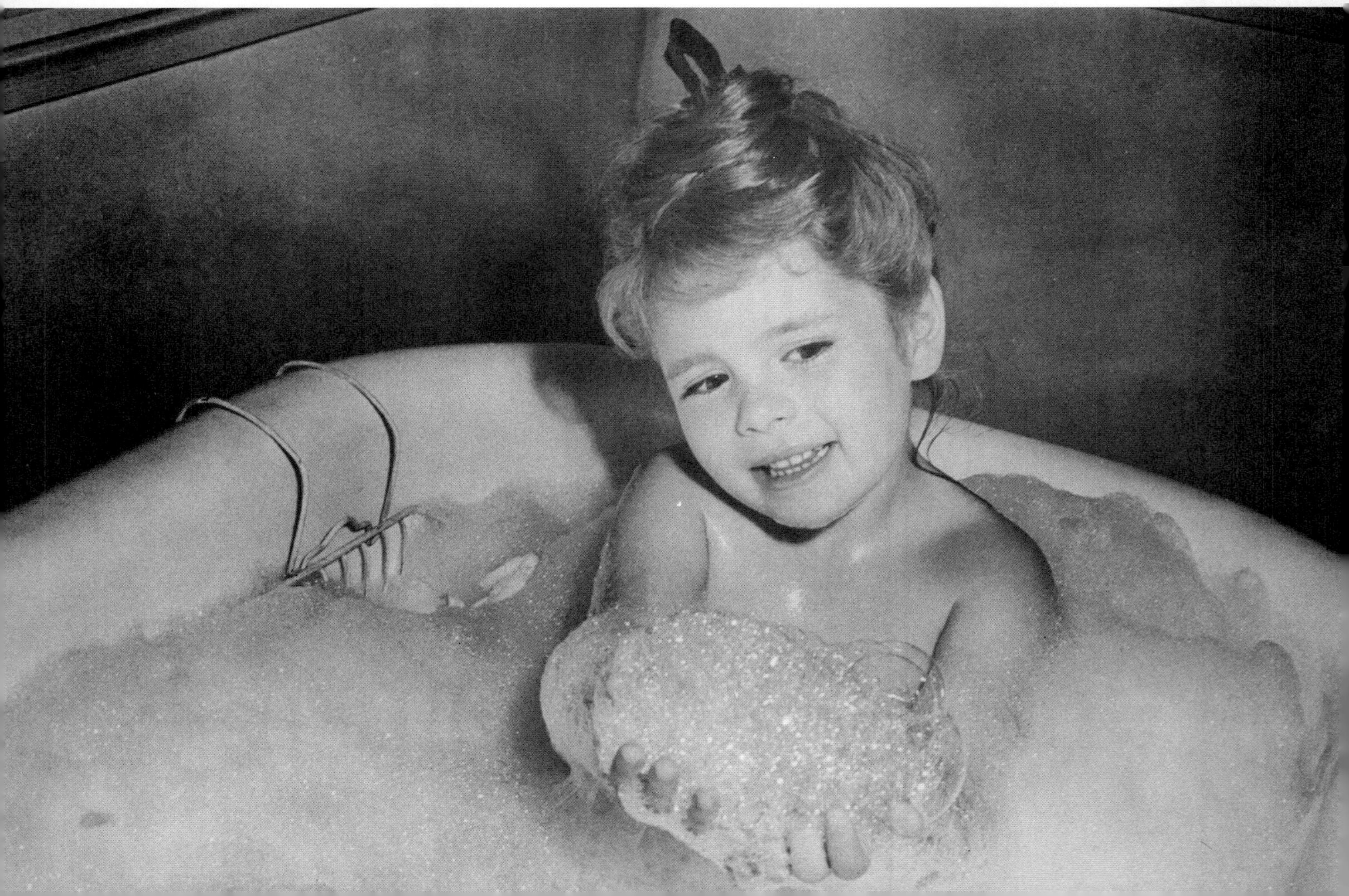

Using a "powder mit," this young Universal-International contract player demonstrates, in a 1946 scene, how to groom oneself after a shower.

Beverly Simmons, a young Universal Pictures actress in the mid-1940s, enjoys a sudsy bath.

Jerry Lewis is shy about taking a bath with girls and children in *The Geisha Boy,* a 1958 Paramount comedy.

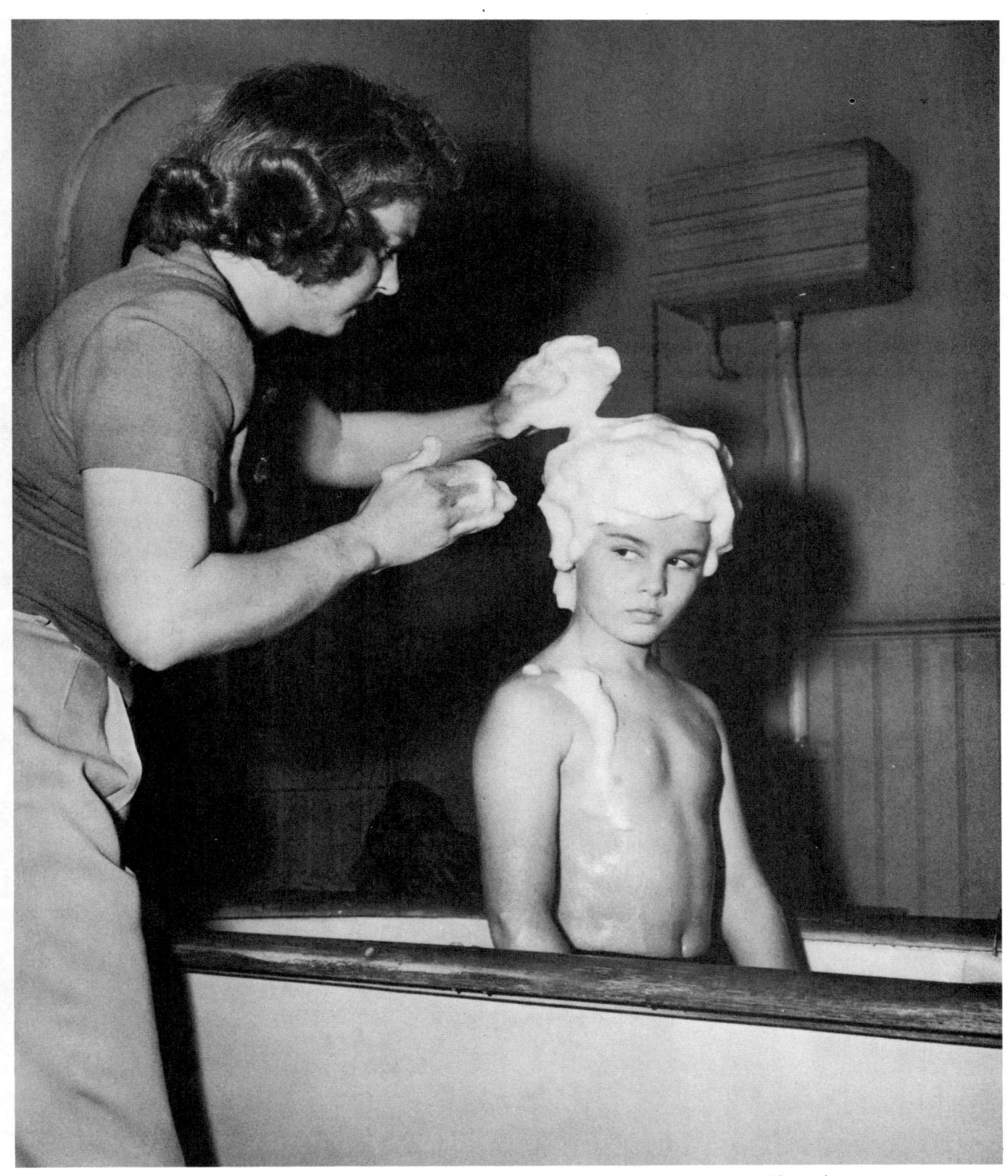
This is Dean Stockwell when he played the lead in RKO Radio's 1948 film, *The Boy With Green Hair*. His hair is being shampooed green!

Famous cowboy star Bill Cody helps Andy Shuford with a bath in a 1920s movie.

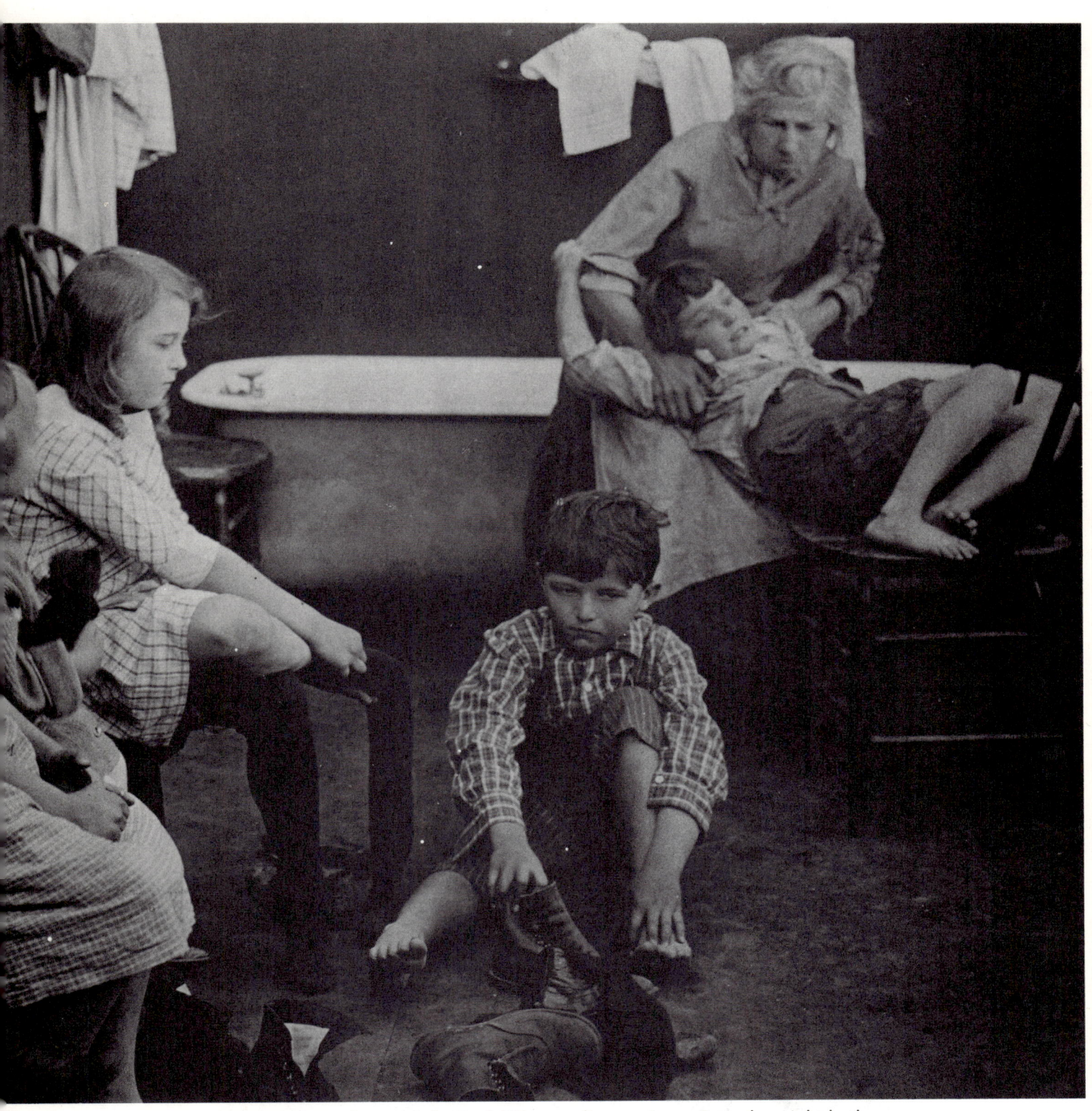
This rare photo shows Violet Radcliff struggling against a Saturday night bath as other Triangle Kiddies await their fate in the 1915 film, *Martha's Vindication*.

Child star Jackie Coogan checks up on a man who doesn't seem to be enjoying his steambath in this silent screen scene from *Buttons*.

Bessie Love soaks her feet in a tub as she talks with movie husband William Haines in *Lovey Mary*.

Carolyn Lee plays a game in the sandbox with a St. Bernard dog between scenes in her supporting role in *Virginia,* a Paramount picture.

(Above) Claudette Colbert gives this girl motherly affection before a bath in the film, *Imitation of Life*.

(Below) Betty Bronson is visited by a very large dog in this scene from the 1925 version of *Peter Pan*.

Rochester has a guest in the bathtub in this scene from *Buck Benny Rides Again,* a Paramount picture starring Jack Benny, Ellen Drew, Andy Devine, Phil Harris and Dennis Day.

Donald Crisp and Kay Walsh attend to the Saturday night ablutions of dog Bobby in Walt Disney's *Greyfriars Bobby,* a 1961 release.

Dorothy Lamour and George Raft take a look at a seal enjoying a bath in *Spawn of the North*.

Shirley Temple bathes her pet, Bitsey, in the 20th Century Fox 1938 film, *Just Around the Corner*.

An ape takes a bath in this scene from *Escape from the Planet of the Apes*. The ape is actress Kim Hunter in ape makeup.

Robert Walker attempts to prove that women are duds as housekeepers, and that's when he finds himself in hot water in *The Skipper Surprised His Wife*, co-starring Joan Leslie. The children are Tommy Myers and Rudy Lee.

Pet dolphin, Flipper, plays with a cap in a *Flipper* television episode on the NBC-TV network in the 1960s. The scene is from a program entitled, *Flipper's Bank Account*.

(Above) Giving this infant his bath are Diana Lewis, Bonita Granville, and Margaret Early. They are students in a wealthy girls' school in MGM's *Forty Little Mothers* (1940), starring Eddie Cantor.

(Below) Robert Benchley demonstrates his technique for bathing a baby in *How to Raise a Baby*, a 1938 MGM movie.

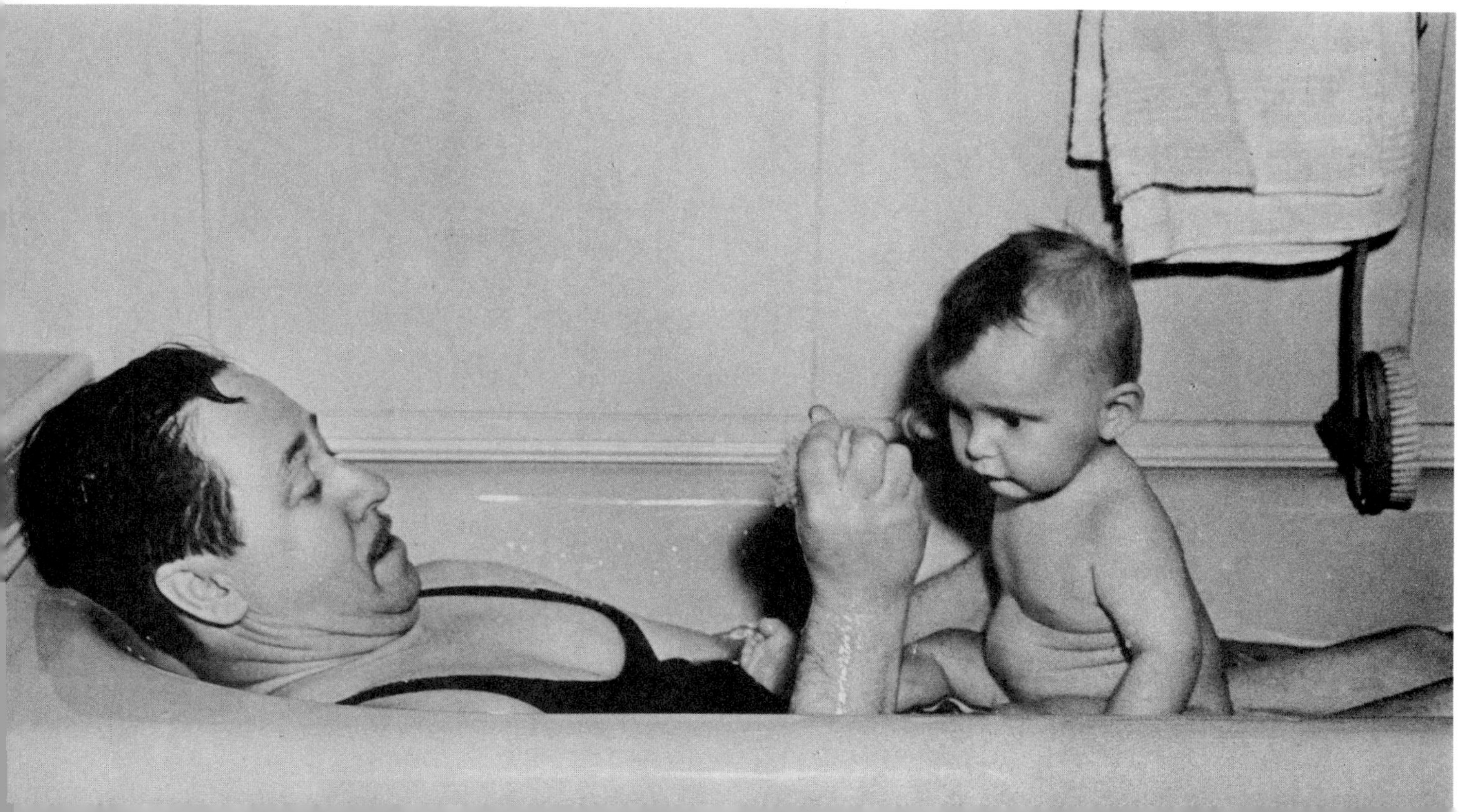

(Above) In this same tub where Shirley Temple often bathed her dolls, she now washes some of the many doll dresses sent to her by children from all parts of the Chicago area. The dresses are exact duplicates of costumes worn by Shirley in different movies.

(Below) James Whitmore and Nancy Davis scrub their screen children Dennis Ross and Nadene Ashdown in MGM's *Rain, Rain, Go Away.*

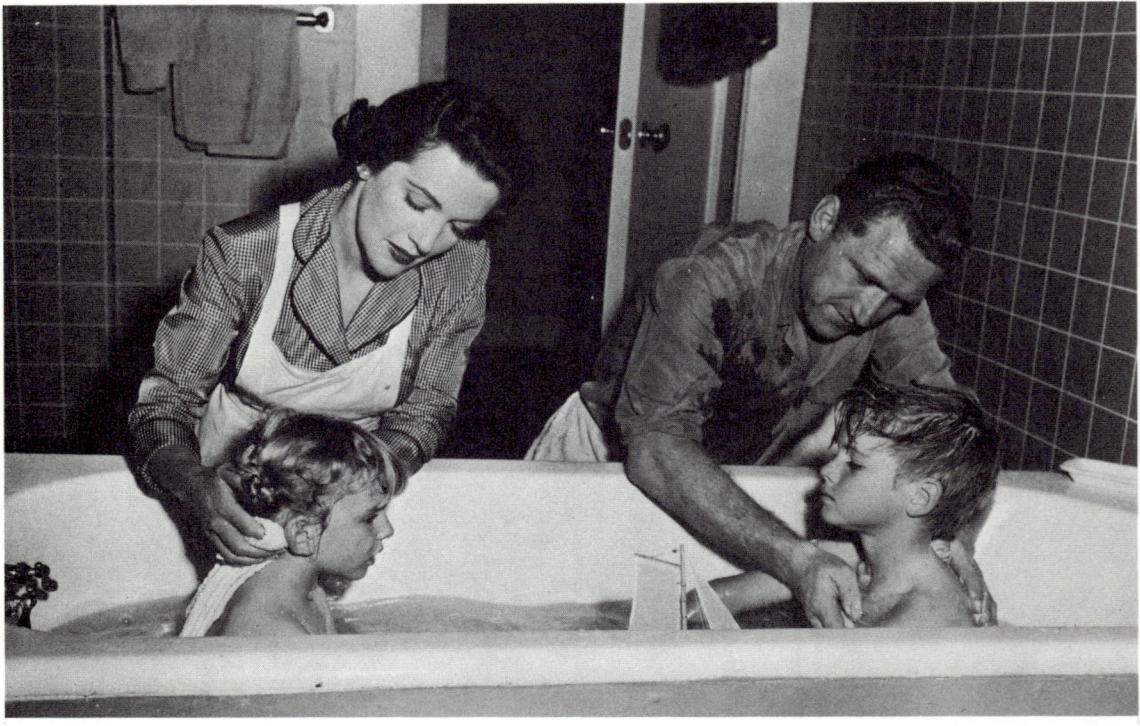

During the filming of a bubble bath scene with Anne Francis, the star's own miniature poodle, Smidgeon, suddenly decided to join his mistress. A still photographer captured the scene, and it was used by MGM to publicize *The Great American Pastime*.

Tom Brown hides his wife and child in the bathroom in this scene from a 1969 Universal Pictures film, *Oh, Johnny, How You Can Love!*

Doris Day is caught in an avalanche of soap suds from the bathroom adjoining her children's room in this scene of comic mischief from the film, *The Thrill of It All,* a 1963 Universal film.

Little Virginia Weidler got her dress dirty just before dinner and takes it upon herself to carry out the threat of her mother to put her under the shower "dress and all." Sister Ann Rutherford looks on in amazement in MGM's *Keeping Company,* which starred Frank Morgan, Irene Rich and Gene Lockhart.

Glenn Ford keeps watch over two enthusiastic "mariners" during this birthday party sequence in *The Courtship of Eddie's Father*, an MGM picture which also starred Shirley Jones and Stella Stevens.

Natalie Wood presides over the baths of her young screen brothers and sisters in this scene from *All the Fine Young Cannibals*, a 1960 release. Robert Wagner and George Hamilton also starred in this 1960 film.

An elephant is given a bath in the film, *The Party,* starring Peter Sellers. It is one of several unusual scenes in the film.

INDEX TO PHOTOGRAPHS

INDEX TO PHOTOGRAPHS

A
Abbott, Bud 125
Alda, Alan 85
Andrews, Julie 98
Arbuckle, Fatty 119
Arlen, Richard 73
Arnaz, Desi 130
Ashdown, Nadene 152

B
Bancroft, Roy 70
Barry, Gene 76
Benchley, Robert 151
Bendix, William 132
Benny, Jack 126
Blondell, Joan 22
Boyd, Jimmy 137
Bracken, Eddie 71
Bremer, Lucille 53
Brent, George 70
Brisson, Lance 136
Bronson, Betty 146
Brown, Joe E. 124
Brown, Tom 153
Burton, Richard 64, 66, 67
Buttons, Red 107

C
Cagney, James 80
Capucine, 107
Chaplin, Charlie 10, 120
Clift, Montgomery 84
Cody, Bill 142
Colbert, Claudette 146
Collins, Joan 54
Connery, Sean 89, 97
Cooper, Gary 72, 95
Coogan, Jackie 144
Costello, Lou 125
Craig, Evon 112
Crawford, Joan 42
Crisp, Donald 147
Crosby, Bing 70
Curtis, Billy 62
Curtis, Tony 110

D
Darnell, Linda 28
Day, Doris 154
Davies, Marion 56
Davies, James 61
Davis, Joan 148
Davis, Nancy 152
De Haven, Gloria 13, 20, 21
De Havilland, Olivia 40
DeMille, Cecil B. 9, 24, 31
Dietrich, Marlene 47
Diller, Phyllis 114
Douglas, Kirk 83
Drew, Ellen 58
Dunaway, Faye 105
Durbin Deanna 33

E
Early, Margaret 151
Eastwood, Clint 62
Ekland, Britt 99
Elg, Taina 54

F
Farrow, Mia 30
Fields, W.C. 133
Fonda, Henry 83, 104
Ford, Glenn 92, 116, 155
Foster, Preston 74
Francis, Ann 153

G
Gable, Clark 103, 118
Garland, Judy 44
Garson, Greer 41
Gardner, Ava 103
Gavin, John 82
Goddard, Paulette 24
Gorcey, Leo 92
Grable, Betty 42
Grant, Cary 109
Granville, Bonita 151

H
Haines, William 144
Hardy, Oliver 122, 123, 124
Hardwicke, Sir Cedric 121
Harlow, Jean 118
Hayward, Susan 37
Hayes, Gabby 129
Hiller, Wendy 60, 117
Hoffman, Dustin 105
Holden, William 78
Holiday, Judy 41
Holloway, Sterling 120
Hope, Bob 113, 114, 131, 132
Horton, Edward Everett 70
Howard, Trevor 117
Hudson, Rock 98
Hume, Benita 117
Hunter, Kim 149
Hussey, Ruth 55

J
Johnson, Rita 55
Johns, Glynis 31, 108

K
Keaton, Buster 121
Kendall, Cy 70
Kerr, Deborah 45, 55
Keyes, Evelyn 36
Kimura, Mitsuko 50
Kirkwood, Jack 131

L
Lahr, Burt 137
Lamour, Dorothy 148
Lancaster, Burt 102
Laurel, Stan 122, 123, 124
Lee, Carolyn 145
Lee, Rudy 149
Lemmon, Jack 63, 92, 112
Lender, Mary Lou 120
Leslie, Joan 149
Lewis, Diana 151
Lewis, Jerry 133, 140
Lloyd, Harold 120
Lollobrigida, Gina 32, 114
Loren, Sophia 39
Love, Bessie 144
Lynn, Diana 118

M
MacDonald, Jeanette 51
Mace, Patricia 56
MacLaine, Shirley 32, 101
Madison, Guy 86
Main, Marjorie 60
Mansfield, Jayne 12, 22, 23
Martin, Dean 101
Martin, Mary 126
Marx, Groucho 127
Marx, Harpo 128
Matthau, Walter 63
Maxwell, Lois 46
McEvoy, J.P. 61
McKinley, J. Edward 90
McNally, Stephen 88
McQueen, Steve 96
Menjou, Adolph 117
Mills, Juliet 112

Mitchum, Robert 69
Monroe, Marilyn 25, 110
Montez, Maria 34
Moran, Lois 48
Moore, Mary Tyler 108
Moore, Victor 93
Murray, Don 74
Myers, Tommy 149

N

Newman, Paul 63, 87
Novak, Kim 26

O

Oakie, Jack 93
Oberon, Merle 58
Olivier, Laurence 82
O'Toole, Peter 64, 65, 66

P

Parker, Punkins 35
Polanski, Roman 106
Powell, William 79
Power, Tyrone 14

R

Radcliff, Violet 143
Raft, George 148
Ralston, Vera 52
Redford, Robert 87
Remick, Lee 102
Rettig, Tommy 138
Reynolds, Burt 75
Reynolds, Debbie 116
Rhoades, Barbara 108
Rochester 147
Rooney, Mickey 134
Ross, Dennis 152
Rowlands, Gena 49
Russell, Jane 18, 19
Russell, Rosalind 42, 136
Rutherford, Ann 154

S

Sanders, George 68
Saunders, Mary Jane 138
Schneider, Maria 15
Schneider, Romy 38
Scott, Randolph 129
Segal, George 98
Sellers, Peter 81, 99, 100, 107, 111
Shearer, Norma 57
Sheridan, Ann 43
Shufford, Andy 142
Simmons, Beverly 139, 140
Simmons, Jean 25
Sinatra, Frank 114
Skelton, Red 130

Smith, Kent 138
Sommer, Elke 114
Stanton, Harry Dean 91
Stockwell, Dean 117, 141
Stroud, Dan 115
St. John, Jill 46
Sullivan, Barry 76
Swanson, Gloria 9

T

Tate, Sharon 106
Taylor, Elizabeth 29, 30
Taylor-Young, Leigh 100
Taylor, Robert 83
Temple, Shirley 148, 152
Three Stooges 126
Treacher, Arthur 74
Turner, Lana 17, 27

V

Van Doren, Mamie 23
Vaughn, Robert 112

W

Wagner, Robert 107, 108
Walker, Robert 149
Walsh, Kay 147
Wayne, John 69, 77
Weidler, Virginia 154
Weld, Tuesday 96
Whitmore, James 152
Williams, Guinn 70
Winters, Shelley 115
Wood, Natalie 35, 135, 155

Y

Young, Gig 80